ARTS & CRAFTS
ART NOUVEAU
ART DECO

ARTS & CRAFTS
ART NOUVEAU
ART DECO

Selections from
the Sydney and Frances Lewis
Decorative Arts Galleries
at the Virginia Museum of Fine Arts

BARRY SHIFMAN

with the assistance of CELESTE FETTA

ARTS AND CRAFTS,
ART NOUVEAU, AND ART DECO
Selections from
the Sydney and Frances Lewis
Decorative Arts Galleries
at the Virginia Museum of Fine Arts

LIBRARY OF CONGRESS CATALOGING-IN-PUBLICATION DATA

Virginia Museum of Fine Arts.
  Arts and Crafts, Art Nouveau, Art Deco : Selections from the Sydney and Frances Lewis
  Decorative Arts Galleries at the Virginia Museum of Fine Arts / Barry Shifman ;
  With the assistance of Celeste Fetta.
    pages cm
Includes index.
  ISBN 978-1-934351-10-9 (alk. paper)
  1. Art objects—Virginia–Richmond—Catalogs. 2. Arts and crafts movement—Catalogs.
3. Decoration and ornament—Art nouveau—Catalogs. 4. Decoration and ornament—
Art deco—Catalogs. 5. Virginia Museum of Fine Arts—Catalogs. I. Shifman, Barry, author.
II. Title. III. Title: Arts and crafts, art nouveau, art deco.
  NK460.R53V548 2015
  745.074′755451–dc23   2015008086

Produced by the Department of Publications
Virginia Museum of Fine Arts
200 N. Boulevard, Richmond, Virginia

Rosalie West, Editor in Chief
Stacy Moore, Project Editor
Sarah Lavicka, Chief Graphic Designer
Travis Fullerton and Katherine Wetzel,
Photographers
Composed and typeset in Futura Std
Printed on acid-free 150 gsm Lumisilk Demi
Matte text by Verona Libri, Verona, Italy

ISBN 978-1-934351-10-9

FRONT COVER: **Punch Bowl with Three Ladles** (detail), 1900, Tiffany Glass and Decorating
Company (American, 1892–1900), p. 43; BACK COVER: **Bracelet with Brooch,** ca. 1925–30,
Raymond Templier (French, 1891–1968), p. 183; FRONTISPIECE: **Corner Cabinet** (detail),
designed 1916, made 1924, Émile-Jacques Ruhlmann (French, 1879–1933), p. 177; CONTENTS and
INDEX: **Panel** (details), designed 1928, made 1929, René Lalique (French, 1860–1945), p. 167

CONTENTS

FOREWORD

The publication of this book coincides with a joyous celebration at the Virginia Museum of Fine Arts (VMFA): the fifth anniversary of an expansion that included the new McGlothlin Wing and reinstallation of the museum's rich and varied permanent collection. These enhancements have allowed us to serve our audience in new and exciting ways.

One of the museum's most important and popular destinations is the Sydney and Frances Lewis Decorative Arts Galleries. These galleries, which are devoted to European and American Arts and Crafts, Art Nouveau, and Art Deco, were reinstalled under the expert supervision of Barry Shifman— author of this book and the Sydney and Frances Lewis Family Curator of Decorative Arts 1890 to the Present.

The frequent appearance of the Lewis name at VMFA is a testament to the importance of this family in the history of the museum. Their support made possible the 1985 West Wing, built to provide space for the collections of modern and contemporary art and decorative arts that Sydney and Frances Lewis donated that same year.

Frances and Sydney donated or funded most of the objects selected for this publication, which also highlights the contributions of other generous patrons. The result is a truly stunning survey of VMFA's decorative arts collection, deemed by many to be one of the most important of its kind in the United States. We hope you will visit the galleries and the museum soon and often!

ALEX NYERGES
Director, Virginia Museum of Fine Arts

ACKNOWLEDGMENTS

With enormous gratitude, I thank Sydney and Frances Lewis for their magnificent contributions to the Virginia Museum of Fine Arts. Their gifts are the cornerstone of our collection of late nineteenth- and early twentieth-century decorative arts. With Mr. Lewis's passing in 1999, Frances Lewis has graciously continued their long history of support. I also wish to acknowledge Dr. Karl and Gisela Kreuzer, Kenneth and Cherie Swenson, and John and Maria Shugars for their contributions to the museum's decorative arts collection.

Among my VMFA colleagues, I am grateful to Alex Nyerges, Director, and Lee Anne Chesterfield, Interim Deputy Director for Art and Education, for their support. I also thank Celeste Fetta, Chief Educator, who worked closely with me on preparing the text for this book. Her keen observations and knowledge of decorative arts are enormously valued. Stacy Moore is to be highly commended for the excellent editing of this volume. Editor in Chief Rosalie West skillfully oversaw the publication process. Sarah Lavicka, Chief Graphic Designer, with whom it has been a pleasure to collaborate, designed this beautiful book. She was assisted by designer Judy Rumble. I also thank Travis Fullerton, Chief Photographer, and Katherine Wetzel, former VMFA photographer, for their superb photography as well as Howell Perkins, Image Rights Licensing Coordinator. The VMFA Shop provided the funds for publication costs, and sales of this book will help support a variety of museum programs.

I also thank Stephen Bonadies, VMFA Deputy Director for Collections and Facilities Management, as well as the Registration Department, including the art handlers. I appreciate the efforts of Kathy Gillis, former Head of Sculpture and Decorative Arts Conservation; Sheila Payaqui, Associate Conservator; and conservators Amy Byrne and Gregory Byrne of Amy Fernandez, Inc.

Finally, I wish to express my sincere appreciation to Dr. Sylvia Yount, former VMFA Chief Curator, for her unflagging encouragement. She was always available to answer questions and offer sage advice.

BARRY SHIFMAN

Until the early 1970s, the Virginia Museum of Fine Arts (VMFA) had few examples of Arts and Crafts, Art Nouveau, or Art Deco objects in its decorative arts collection. Instead, the focus of the collection was European and American objects made before 1880 (with the exception of the late nineteenth-century Russian collection of Lillian Thomas Pratt, donated to the museum in 1947). In 1971, however, the museum mounted an exhibition of Art Nouveau drawn from public and private sources, including objects from Sydney and Frances Lewis of Richmond (fig. 1). The Lewises had recently begun to form their own personal collection of Art Nouveau, and they responded enthusiastically to VMFA's request for loans. Then, the next year, they gave the museum $500,000 for Art Nouveau acquisitions—the first of many generous steps that led to the creation of VMFA's internationally renowned collection of decorative arts dating from about 1880 to 1935.

Sydney and Frances Lewis began collecting art during the time they were operating Best Products Company, one of America's largest chains of catalogue-showroom stores, which they had founded in 1957 (it closed in the late 1990s). According to Frances Lewis, the couple initially sought eighteenth-century English furniture but soon realized that most great works were already in museums or owned by individuals. The Lewises then turned to contemporary art and met the Abstract Expressionist painter Theodoros Stamos, who owned glass by Louis Comfort Tiffany and Art Nouveau furniture by other masters. Stamos convinced the Lewises that it was still

Fig. 1: Sydney and Frances Lewis, 1987

Fig. 2: French Art Nouveau Gallery, VMFA

possible to find superb examples of late nineteenth-century decorative arts. He introduced them to Lillian Nassau, then the only major American dealer specializing in Art Nouveau, and took them to auction houses that were selling objects from the era. At one of these auctions, in 1971, the Lewises acquired their first example of Art Nouveau furniture. Later that same year, Frederick Brandt—at the time VMFA's curator of twentieth-century art—organized the museum's 1971 Art Nouveau exhibition and began to work with the Lewises in forming their collection. In 1976, the museum created a gallery devoted to Art Nouveau—the first in the United States. The Lewises' collection, which grew to encompass Arts and Crafts as well as Art Deco objects, eventually included masterpieces by Peter Behrens, Eileen Gray, Hector Guimard, Josef Hoffmann, Charles Rennie Mackintosh, Louis Majorelle, Émile-Jacques Ruhlmann, Louis Comfort Tiffany, Frank Lloyd Wright, and numerous other artists of the late nineteenth and early twentieth centuries.

In 1985, the Lewises' generosity culminated in the donation of their entire decorative arts collection—along with modern paintings and sculpture—to VMFA. Earlier, in May 1981, Mr. Lewis had executed a deed of gift for $6 million, of which $2 million was "to provide for a permanent endowment for the collections, and the remainder . . . for the new wing to house the collections." Frederick Brandt supervised the installation of the Sydney and Frances Lewis Galleries in the new wing and wrote a book, *Late 19th and 20th Century Decorative Arts,* featuring one hundred objects from the new galleries. After Brandt's retirement from the museum in 1996, two separate curatorial departments were created from the former twentieth-century art division: the Department of Art after 1900 and the Department of Decorative Arts after 1890. Brandt later served as a consulting curator of decorative arts until his death in 2007. In 2001, Frances Lewis (whose husband had passed away in 1999) expressed her intent to endow the two curatorial positions, and the funds were received in 2004. Brandt's oversight and care of the Sydney and Frances Lewis collection of decorative arts—as well as the Lewis collection of modern and contemporary paintings and sculpture—represent an impressive curatorial achievement.

A new installation of decorative arts in the Sydney and Frances Lewis Galleries opened to the public in May 2010, more than twenty-five years after the galleries were inaugurated. More than 90 percent of the objects now on view are gifts donated by the Lewises, and many of the acquisitions were funded through the Sydney and Frances Lewis Endowment Fund. Also on display in the galleries is a selection from another personal collection, which was acquired by Frederick Brandt in 2002 from Karl and Gisela Kreuzer of Munich: a unique group of approximately five hundred American and European buckles, related necklaces, belts, and buttons dating from about 1890 to 1910. There are now more than four hundred decorative arts objects from 1880 to 1935 on view in the Lewis galleries (figs. 2–3), arranged by country and style: American Arts and Crafts; Louis Comfort Tiffany and Tiffany Studios (glass, lamps, mosaics, metalwork, a leaded-glass window, and jewelry); British Arts and Crafts; Austrian and German Arts and Crafts; French Art Nouveau; and French Art Deco.

Since 1985, when Mr. Brandt published the first catalogue on the Lewis galleries, the museum has made numerous acquisitions; many are on display for the first time in the Lewis galleries and are included in this book. During my own curatorial tenure at VMFA, which began in 2007, the museum has acquired several major works of art with the Lewis endowment, including an oil-on-canvas design for a tapestry (*The Fairy Caprice*) by Georges de Feure; an important French Art Deco ceramic vase by René Buthaud; and a rare group of seventeen photographs documenting the interior decoration and furnishings of Studio Saint-James, fashion designer Jacques Doucet's residence in the suburbs of Paris. We are pleased to present highlights of the museum's collection in this beautifully illustrated volume.

BARRY SHIFMAN
Sydney and Frances Lewis Family Curator of Decorative Arts
1890 to the Present

Fig. 3: French Art Deco Gallery, VMFA

In an attempt to improve standards of living and design, artists in Victorian England embraced the Arts and Crafts ideology. This movement, which affected all aspects of society, was based on the theories of art critic John Ruskin and designer William Morris. Their shared philosophy condemned the use of machines in the creation of everyday objects, espoused the beauty and value of handcraftsmanship, and stressed the importance of nature as a source of personal and artistic expression.

Arts and Crafts practitioners applied these ideals to the creation of objects such as furniture, metalwork, jewelry, textiles, and ceramics throughout Great Britain, Europe, and the United States. A major aspect of the Arts and Crafts movement championed by Ruskin was the formation of workshops based on medieval guilds, including the Century Guild, established in England by Arthur Mackmurdo in 1882, and the Guild of Handicraft, founded in 1888 by Charles Robert Ashbee.

BRITISH ARTS and CRAFTS

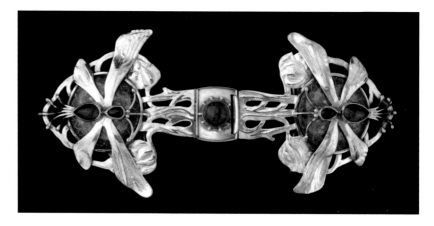

CHARLES ROBERT ASHBEE
British, 1863–1942
Made by GUILD OF HANDICRAFT
British (London and Chipping Campden),
1888–1908

Buckle or Cloak Clasp, ca. 1900
Silver, enamel, amethysts
2 1/2 x 5 7/16 x 11/16 in. (6.35 x 13.8 x 1.75 cm)
Gift of Sydney and Frances Lewis,
85.223a–b

Charles Robert Ashbee was one of the major architects and designers of the British Arts and Crafts movement. Like others who embraced the Arts and Crafts ideology, he believed that handcraftsmanship was crucial in the creation of objects such as furniture, metalwork, and jewelry. Inspired by medieval guilds, Ashbee founded the Guild of Handicraft in London's East End in 1888. He operated this organization on the principle that the individual contributions of the artist, designer, and craftsman were equally valuable, a major tenet of the Arts and Crafts philosophy. By the end of the nineteenth century, Ashbee's guild included nineteen cabinetmakers and fifteen metalworkers, as well as other members.

An important component of the guild's metalwork and jewelry was wirework, of which this buckle or cloak clasp is an example. The guild displayed such pieces at the Arts and Crafts Exhibition Society in London, formed in 1887 to promote the public exhibition of decorative objects. ∎

WILLIAM A. S. BENSON
British, 1854–1924
Made by W.A.S. BENSON AND
COMPANY, LTD.
British (London), 1880–1920

Fire Screen, 1891
Copper, brass
35 ¼ x 21 x 9 ½ in. (89.5 x 53.3 x 24.1 cm)
Marked (back): *REG. NO 181516: W.A.S. /
BENSON*
Gift of Frederick R. Brandt in memory of
Carol J. Brandt, 2004.78a–b

William Benson was a pioneer of modern design, an innovator in
technology, and a master of metalwork. He is especially known for his
unique copper lighting fixtures. Although a participant in the British Arts
and Crafts movement, which prioritized handcraftsmanship, Benson used
machines in his production. For this fire screen, he combined copper and
brass in both cast and stamped forms to create a complex group of curling
vanes that resemble leaves or petals. According to a period photograph,
a similar fire screen was in the drawing room at Windleshaw House,
Benson's East Sussex residence. ▪

Walter Crane, one of the most important designers of the late nineteenth century, created the decoration on this charger. A key participant in the Anglo-American Aesthetic movement, which celebrated the idea of "art for the art's sake," and a leading exponent of the British Arts and Crafts movement, Crane designed book illustrations, stained-glass windows, wallpaper, ceramics, and textiles. This depiction of Saint George and the Dragon relates to his illustration in an 1894 publication of Edmund Spenser's *The Faerie Queene*. The plate's decorative inscription reads: *Un chevalier Sans Peur et Sans Reproche* (A Knight Without Fear and Without Reproach). On the back, Tudor roses were painted in gold and ruby colors.

All of Crane's designs for Pilkington Tile and Pottery Company were executed in Lancastrian Lustre, named for Lancaster County, England, where the company was located. "Lustre" describes the pearly sheen on the pottery's surface, which was achieved by first applying a glaze of various materials, including metallic oxides and red clay, and then varying the temperature during the firing process. Several ceramic chargers with Crane's chivalric design were made at Pilkington's using different color palettes.

WALTER CRANE
British, 1845–1915
Decorated by RICHARD JOYCE
British, 1873–1931
Made by PILKINGTON TILE AND POTTERY COMPANY
British (Clifton Junction, Manchester), 1893–1957

Charger, designed 1904–6, made 1912
Earthenware, gold and ruby luster
19 in. (48.2 cm) diam.
Inscribed (front): monogram of Walter Crane; (back): monogram of Richard Joyce
Marked (back): P[ilkington] / XII[1912] / ENGLAND / 2477 / +

Funds given in honor of Frederick R. Brandt by The Council of the Virginia Museum of Fine Arts, Nancy and Raymond Hunt, Dr. John M. Alexander and Mrs. Helen Inconstanti Alexander, the Brownell Family, the Sydney and Frances Lewis Endowment Fund, and Swenson Art Nouveau Fund, 2011.8

Alexander Fisher, painter, sculptor, silversmith, and enameler, was a major contributor to the British Arts and Crafts movement. He was also a distinguished teacher and director of the enameling division at the Central School of Arts and Crafts in London from 1896 to 1898. Fisher's own enamels, which make up a large part of his work, include panels,

ALEXANDER FISHER
British, 1864–1936

Tristan and Isolde Buckle, 1894
Nickel silver, enamel, opals
4 ¼ x 6 ⅞ in. (10.80 x 17.46 cm)
(two parts)
Inscribed (front, on enamel): *Alex. Fisher, AF 94*
Marked (front, in the silver): *Tristan Isolde*
Adolph D. and Wilkins C. Williams Fund, 2002.35a–b

triptychs, and jewelry such as belts, buckles, and pendants. He showed these objects regularly at the Royal Academy, the Arts and Crafts Exhibition Society, and several international exhibitions. His process involved adding multiple layers of translucent enamel to a foil base, giving his works the illusion of depth.

This buckle, enameled with scenes from the Arthurian legend of Tristan and Isolde, is one of the most outstanding examples of Fisher's work. It was on display at the Royal Academy in London in 1894. ■

EDWARD W. GODWIN
British, 1833–1886
Made by WILLIAM WATT
British (London), active 1867–1885

Cabinet, 1869
Ebonized wood, metal, silver
97 3/4 x 65 x 179 in. (243.8 x 165.1 x
454.7 cm)
Sydney and Frances Lewis Endowment Fund,
92.2a–b

Fig. 4: **Chair**, 1877, Edward W. Godwin;
made by William Watt, mahogany, cane,
38 3/16 x 16 5/16 x 16 in. (97 x 41.4 x 40.6
cm). Gift of Mr. David K. E. Bruce; the Estate
of Mrs. Edna Grumbach; Miss Elsie Murphy;
John Barton Payne; Mrs. E. A. Rennolds in
memory of Mr. and Mrs. John Kerr Branch;
Mr. Raphael Stora; and bequest of John C.
and Florence S. Goddin, by exchange;
with additional funds from the Arthur and
Margaret Glasgow Fund, 96.99

The Aesthetic movement, which spanned the 1870s and 1880s in Great
Britain and the United States, celebrated the idea that domestic objects
should be both useful and beautiful. Influenced by international cultures—
particularly of the Far East—as well as natural forms, the style introduced
eclecticism to late nineteenth-century design.

This cabinet, one of about seven related versions made by William Watt,
was commissioned by London lawyer Charles Lane from the architect
and designer Edward Godwin. Godwin was among the first artists in
England to promote a Japanesque style in both furniture design and
interior decoration. The ebonized wood of the cabinet, the gallery at the
top, and the grid pattern of the facade reveal Godwin's pioneering interest
in Asian art. A later chair designed by Godwin (fig. 4), also in VMFA's
collection, suggests his interest in combining Japanese and historic English
motifs in furniture. ■

Attributed to ARCHIBALD KNOX
British (Isle of Man), 1864–1933
Made by W. H. HASELER, LTD.
British (Birmingham), 1848/49–1946
For LIBERTY AND COMPANY
British (London), founded 1875

Mirror, 1902–3
Silver, enamel, wood, mirrored glass
18 ¾ x 8 ⅞ x ½ in. (47.6 x 22.5 x 1.2 cm)
Marked (front, lower left): *L & C*, Birmingham
city mark, lion passant, *c*, *CYMRIC*
Gift of Sydney and Frances Lewis, 85.177

Archibald Knox was an Arts and Crafts designer, calligrapher, water-colorist, and teacher. Born on the Isle of Man, he was inspired in his design by the region's crosses—commemorative stones that incorporated interlaced Celtic motifs and mythological forms. In 1897 Knox began working for the Silver Studio, which for several years sold his designs for metalwork, jewelry, garden ornaments, and textiles to the famous London department store Liberty and Company. Knox was also the primary designer for Liberty's Cymric and Tudric lines of metalwork.

VMFA's unique tabletop mirror is attributed to Knox based on its marks, rarity, and design. Because of their complexity and high cost, very few large pieces of Cymric were actually made. This rare mirror is decorated with a botanical motif that is found in Celtic art and one that Knox used in other examples of his Cymric metalwork. The museum also has more than twenty belts and buckles made after designs by Knox for Liberty. ■

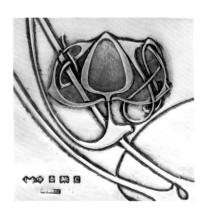

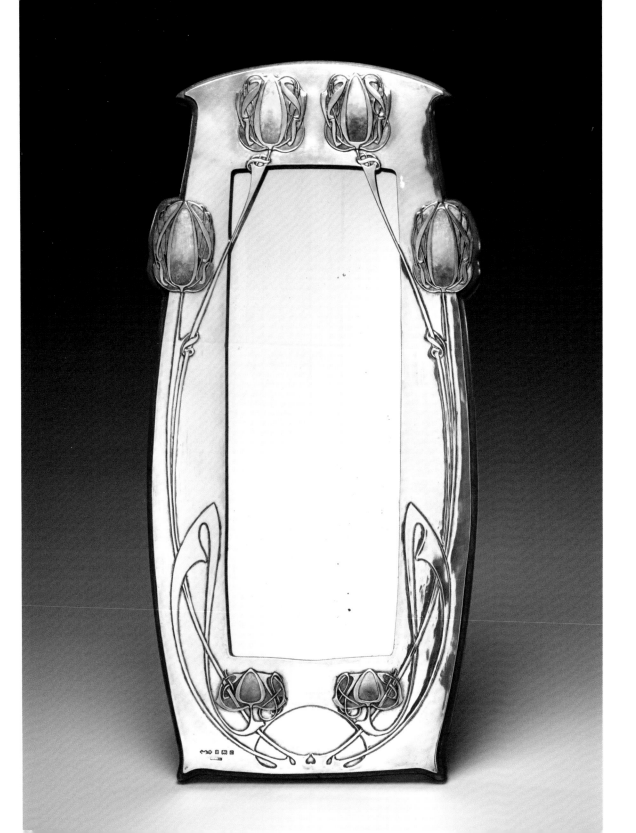

MARGARET MACDONALD MACKINTOSH
Scottish, 1865–1933

Four Queens, 1909
Wood, paint, gesso
22 ⅞ x 15 ¾ in. (58.1 x 40 cm) (each)
Inscribed (each panel, lower right): *MMM / 1909*
Gift of Sydney and Frances Lewis, 85.143.1–4

Margaret Macdonald Mackintosh, wife of Scottish architect Charles Rennie Mackintosh, created stenciled and gessoed pictures for the tearooms that her husband designed for Catherine Cranston in Glasgow. Later, Macdonald Mackintosh assisted her husband in the interior decoration of Hous'hill, Cranston's Glasgow residence. These four panels, originally set into the walls of the Card Room at Hous'hill, depict the queens of the four card suits flanked by two court pages. Macdonald Mackintosh's use of gesso to create a high-relief linear style was characteristic of her work during the period.

CHARLES RENNIE MACKINTOSH
Scottish, 1868–1928
Made by FRANCIS SMITH AND SON
Scottish (Glasgow), active 1893–1952

Chair, 1898
Oak, rush
53 ¾ x 18 x 17 ¾ in. (136.5 x 47.6 x 45.1 cm)
Sydney and Frances Lewis Art Nouveau Fund, 79.29

Charles Rennie Mackintosh is considered one of the outstanding architect-designers of the late nineteenth century. He was the principal contributor to the Arts and Crafts movement in Scotland and collaborated with three other Scottish artists—his wife, Margaret Macdonald Mackintosh; her sister Frances MacDonald; and Herbert McNair. Known collectively as the Glasgow Four, the group created a unique style for posters, metalwork, interior decoration, and other works of art. In 1896 Mackintosh won the competition to design and furnish the Glasgow School of Art, believed to be his finest building and a major achievement in modern architecture. His use of geometry was very influential, most notably with the artists of the Vienna Secession.

One of the architect's active patrons was Catherine Cranston, the originator and owner of a number of tearooms throughout Glasgow. Aiming to provide a quiet place where one could have tea or a friendly chat, Miss Cranston's tearooms, perhaps owing to Mackintosh's interior decoration and furnishings, were a great success.

This chair is one of a group that Mackintosh designed for the Crown Luncheon Room, Catherine Cranston's Argyle Street tearoom, his first significant commission for interior design. Unusual in form and design, the chairs are now among Mackintosh's best-known models and are considered icons of British Arts and Crafts furniture. The tall back, which provided some privacy for the sitter, also served an architectural function within the space. Mackintosh decorated his own house with chairs of this model. ■

Between 1903 and 1919, Charles Rennie Mackintosh created the interior decoration and furnishings for Hous'hill, the Glasgow residence of Catherine Cranston. One of the distinctive spaces of the house was the drawing room (fig. 5), also known as the music room, for which this armchair was made. The importance of this sculptural piece lies in its aesthetics rather than its function or comfort. The vertical slats echoed a curved screen that was a key architectural feature in the room, and the dark-stained wood and oval mauve-colored glass insets contrasted with the white walls. Other pieces of furniture designed by Mackintosh for the drawing room at Hous'hill are in the collection at VMFA, including an ebonized-wood tea table and a wrought-iron fire front. ▪

CHARLES RENNIE MACKINTOSH
Scottish, 1868–1928
Made by ALEX MARTIN
Scottish (Glasgow), active 1898–1909
Glass by McCULLOCH AND COMPANY
Scottish (Glasgow), active 1892–1925

Armchair, 1904
Stained wood, glass, replacement fabric
47 x 24 ½ x 25 in. (119.3 x 61.5 x 63.5 cm)
Gift of Sydney and Frances Lewis, 85.145

Fig. 5: Interior decoration and furnishings designed by Charles Rennie Mackintosh for the drawing room at Hous'hill, Glasgow, Scotland, 1904. The Hunterian, University of Glasgow, 2015

CHARLES RENNIE MACKINTOSH
Scottish, 1868–1928

Mantel Clock, 1917
Ebonized wood, ivory, Erinoid, French
clockworks
9 11/32 x 5 1/8 x 4 7/16 in. (23.7 x 13 x 11.3 cm)
Gift of Sydney and Frances Lewis, 85.222

In 1916 Charles Rennie Mackintosh was commissioned by W. J. Bassett-Lowke to refurbish his townhouse in Northampton, England. Bassett-Lowke was a member of the Design and Industries Association, founded in 1915 to introduce good design to everyday machine-made objects. This clock is among the pieces that Mackintosh designed for the house; it appears in contemporary photographs of the dining room. The clock-face numbers are inlaid in ivory on a central panel of green Erinoid, an early synthetic material made from resin or protein plastic. Bassett-Lowke's house was the final commission for Mackintosh, who later moved to France, where he spent the remainder of his life. ■

In 1882 architect and designer Arthur Mackmurdo founded the Century Guild, a group of Arts and Crafts artists who made handcrafted objects. Inspired by the teachings of John Ruskin, it was the first such guild to succeed in Great Britain. Although numerous examples of furniture, graphics, and metalwork were designed by Mackmurdo for the guild, this chair is the best known. There were presumably six or eight chairs of this design made by Collinson and Lock for the Century Guild. Although the form is based on eighteenth-century English furniture, the row of curvilinear tendrils and flowers on the back splat is one of the first examples of the Art Nouveau style, which spread throughout Europe and the United States. ▪

ARTHUR HEYGATE MACKMURDO
British, 1851–1942
Made by COLLINSON AND LOCK
British (London), 1870–1897
For CENTURY GUILD
British (London), 1882–1888

Chair, ca. 1882–83
Mahogany, paint, leather
38 ½ x 19 ½ x 18 ½ in. (97.5 x 49.5 x 47 cm)
Inscribed (bottom, back left): *C. G.*
Sydney and Frances Lewis Endowment Fund, 2003.8

Designed and painted by CHARLES
VOYSEY
British, 1857–1941
Probably made by FREDERICK COOTE
British, active 1878–1906

Mantel Clock, designed 1895,
made ca. 1896–1901
Wood, paint, brass, clockworks
19 11/16 x 10 5/8 x 7 in. (50 x 27 x 17 cm)
Inscribed (on clockworks): *Mary, Countess
of Lovelace/Ockham Park/Ockham*
Gift of Sydney and Frances Lewis, 85.217

Like many of his contemporaries, architect Charles Voysey designed
buildings as well as their furnishings. This clock was initially owned by
Mary, Countess of Lovelace, an Arts and Crafts enthusiast who, with her
husband, commissioned designs from the architect for their house at
Ockham Park, Surrey, in 1894. The body of the clock, which Voysey
himself painted, features a landscape with three stylized trees before
a floral field. The phrase *Time & Tide Wait For No Man* is painted on a
ribbon at the center of the clock. The numerals are formed from the Latin
phrase *tempus fugit* (time flies). Voysey displayed a clock like this one at
the Arts and Crafts Exhibition Society in London in 1896. An identical
example was also at his own house, The Orchard, which was under
construction at Chorleywood in England in 1899. ■

Rejecting the curving lines that characterized European Art Nouveau, certain artists in the United States created a straightforward American style free of excessive decoration. From coast to coast, they chose to emphasize the inherent construction of an object through simplicity of design. The American Arts and Crafts movement, based on the ideas promoted by British theorists John Ruskin and William Morris, embraced the philosophy that handmade creations are more significant than machine-made objects.

Perhaps the most influential of the Arts and Crafts designers on the East Coast was Gustav Stickley, who created the idea of the "Craftsman" house and published *The Craftsman* magazine. To achieve total artistic unity, Stickley also designed and manufactured various accessory objects for his interiors. He chose American oak for his furniture, which he finished in warm, mellow tones that would complement other wood, leather, and metal objects. Another important force in the East was Elbert Hubbard, who established the Roycroft community in East Aurora, New York, in 1893. This group of artists created books, metalwork, and furniture based on Arts and Crafts principles.

One of the best-known architects associated with the Arts and Crafts movement in the Midwest was Frank Lloyd Wright. The rectilinear simplicity of Wright's furniture is reminiscent of Stickley's, although it also reflects the distinct architecture he produced during this period. Brothers Charles and Henry Greene worked in Pasadena, California. Their buildings, interior decoration, and furnishings were inspired by the simplicity and fine craftsmanship of Asian design. Other artists on the West Coast developed the Arts and Crafts movement in cities such as San Francisco and Los Angeles.

AMERICAN ARTS and CRAFTS

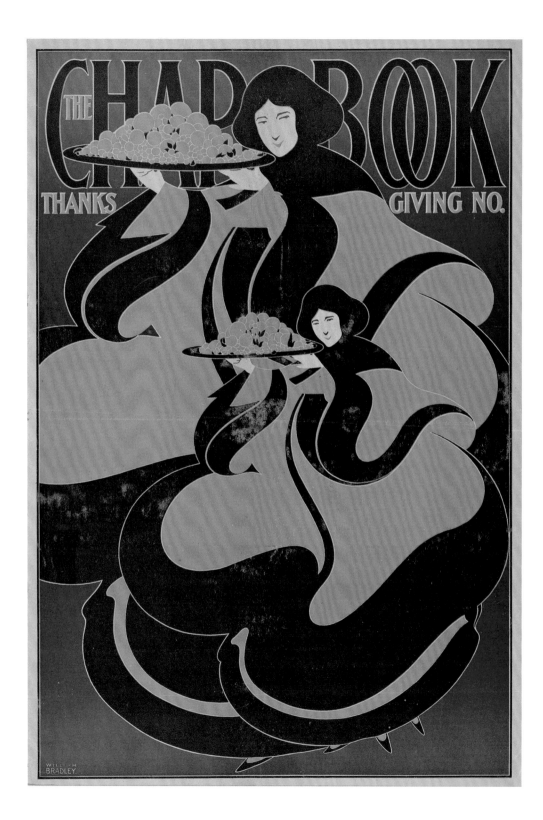

WILL H. BRADLEY
American, 1868–1962
Published by STONE AND KIMBALL
American (Boston and Chicago),
1893–1897

The Chap-Book, Thanksgiving Number, 1894
Lithograph
20 x 13 ¾ in. (50.8 x 34.9 cm)
Inscribed: *WILL H. / BRADLEY*
Sydney and Frances Lewis Art Nouveau Fund,
74.5.1

WILL H. BRADLEY
American, 1868–1962
Published by CHARLES SCRIBNER'S
SONS
American (New York, New York),
founded 1846

The Modern Poster, 1895
Lithograph
19 ⅜ x 11 ⅝ in. (49.2 x 29.5 cm)
Inscribed: *WILL H. / BRADLEY 95*
Arthur and Margaret Glasgow Fund and
Sydney and Frances Lewis Endowment Fund,
90.36

VMFA has more than 120 late nineteenth-century American advertising posters by Will Bradley, Arthur Wesley Dow, Maxfield Parrish, Louis John Rhead, and other artists. Bradley's first poster, *The Twins*, was created in 1894 for Stone and Kimball's publication *The Chap-Book*. His posters of 1894–95, including these works, are among the earliest examples in the American Arts and Crafts style that also suggest the influence of Art Nouveau. By his mid-twenties, Bradley was among the most successful art-poster designers in the United States.

One of the major contributions to American art pottery was Fulper Pottery Company's Vasekraft line, which was first available in 1909. For the next twenty years, the firm made Vasekraft objects with unusual shapes and glazes. This lamp, with a hand-thrown base and shade, has a distinctive green glaze created by Fulper. Several advertisements in period magazines noted that the Vasekraft line, especially the lamps, were "the latest in interior decoration, [adding] beauty to every home." One journal extolled the lamps' "originality and beauty of design" and "wonderful workmanship." ■

FULPER POTTERY COMPANY
American (Flemington, New Jersey),
1860–ca. 1935

Lamp, ca. 1915–18
Stoneware, glass, electrical parts
18 x 13 in. (45.7 x 33 cm)
Marked (bottom): *FULPER*
Gift of Sydney and Frances Lewis,
85.150a–b

**FURNITURE SHOP
OF THE ROYCROFTERS**
American (East Aurora, New York),
1895–1938

Bookcase, ca. 1905–10
Oak, copper, paint, glass
65 ¾ x 55 ¼ x 15 ¾ in. (167 x 140.3 x
40 cm)
Marked (front, center): Roycroft orb; *R*;
cross mark
Gift of Sydney and Frances Lewis, 85.69

Elbert Hubbard was one of the best-known leaders of the American Arts
and Crafts movement. In 1893 he founded the Roycroft community in East
Aurora, New York, a suburb of Buffalo. This group was loosely inspired
by medieval guilds, such as those valued by William Morris, one of the
leading practitioners of the Arts and Crafts movement in Great Britain.
The artists and craftsmen of Roycroft created books, metalwork, furniture,
and other objects. Their furniture is recognized for its simplicity of line and
structural detail, as seen in the mortise-and-tenon construction on the sides
of this bookcase. An orb surmounted with a cross, the mark of the
Roycrofters, is clearly evident on the front of this piece.

From 1907 to 1909 architects Charles and Henry Greene designed bungalows for wealthy American clients on the West Coast. The first house they completed during this period was owned by Robert Blacker, a retired lumberman, in Pasadena, California. The Blacker house is the Greenes' largest and most important commission. It reflected their interest in Japanese art, evident in the overhanging timber construction, lanterns, and refined furniture. This sideboard, created for the dining room (fig. 6), is one of the Greenes' masterpieces given its scale, finely carved mahogany, and details of ebony, copper, pewter, and mother-of-pearl. In the Blacker home, the sideboard was flanked by a pair of chairs and wall lights, also in VMFA's collection. ■

Fig. 6: Dining room designed
by the Greene brothers for the
Robert Blacker House, Pasadena,
California, ca. 1907–9. Courtesy
Avery Architectural and Fine Art
Library, Columbia University

CHARLES SUMNER GREENE
American, 1868–1957
HENRY MATHER GREENE
American, 1870–1954
Made by HALL MANUFACTURING
COMPANY
American (Pasadena, California),
1906–1922

Sideboard, ca. 1907–9

Mahogany, ebony, copper, pewter, mother-
of-pearl
38 ⅛ x 95 ¼ x 22 ¼ in. (96.8 x 241.9 x
56.5 cm)
Sydney and Frances Lewis Endowment Fund,
93.16

One of a Pair of Wall Lights,
ca. 1907–9

Mahogany, ebony, electrical fittings,
replacement fabric
18 ½ x 11 ¾ x 7 ¼ in. (46.9 x 29.8 x
18.4 cm)
Sydney and Frances Lewis Endowment Fund,
93.17.1–2

Pair of Chairs, ca. 1907–9

Mahogany, ebony, copper, pewter, mother-
of-pearl, replacement upholstery
42 ¼ x 20 x 20 ¼ in. (107 x 50.8 x
51.4 cm) (each)
Gift of the Sydney and Frances Lewis
Foundation, by exchange, 97.122.1–2

GRUEBY FAIENCE COMPANY
American (Boston, Massachusetts),
ca. 1897–1909

Vase, ca. 1900
Stoneware
22 ¼ x 9 in. (56.5 x 22.8 cm)
Marked (bottom): *GRUEBY FAIENCE COMPANY*
BOSTON U.S.A.
Inscribed (bottom): *KY*
Arthur and Margaret Glasgow Fund, 90.118

The Grueby Faience Company was one of the largest
makers of Arts and Crafts pottery in the United States.
Founder William Grueby developed matte glazes in
greens, yellows, blues, and ivory that changed the
appearance of American art pottery. George Prentiss
Kendrick, who designed this vase and its decoration,
was responsible for most of Grueby's early designs,
which the company continued to produce for many
years. Like other commercial manufacturers, Grueby
standardized its pottery forms, and men were hired to
make the objects while women art students decorated
them according to company designs. This vase, similar
to an example displayed at the 1900 Exposition
Universelle in Paris and the 1904 Louisiana Purchase
Exposition in Saint Louis, is impressive in both size
and the quality of glazing and decoration. It was
executed by the Japanese artist Kiichi Yamada, who
was active at Grueby from 1900 to 1902. ▪

The Furniture Shop in San Francisco was a unique Arts and Crafts partner-ship between husband and wife, Arthur and Lucia Mathews. Arthur was the chief designer and oversaw mural decoration, furniture, and interiors. Lucia carved, decorated, and painted furniture and other objects, such as this covered jar, which she gave to her sister as a wedding gift. Although there are a number of similar jars in existence, each one differs slightly in appearance.

LUCIA K. MATHEWS
American, 1870–1955
Made by FURNITURE SHOP
American (San Francisco, California),
1906–1920

Covered Jar, ca. 1906
Wood, paint, gilding
12 ½ x 10 in. (31.7 x 25.4 cm) diam.
Inscribed (frieze band): *Lucia K. Mathews*
Gift of the Sydney and Frances Lewis
Foundation, 85.299a–b

LOUIS JOHN RHEAD
British (active in the United States),
1857–1926
Printed by LIEBLER AND MAASS
LITHOGRAPHERS
American (New York, New York)

Morning Journal, 1895
Lithograph
48 ⅝ x 60 in. (123.4 x 152.4 cm)
Inscribed: *L.J.R.*
Arthur and Margaret Glasgow Fund and
Sydney and Frances Lewis Endowment
Fund, 90.92

Born in Great Britain, Louis John Rhead studied at the famed South Kensington Art School. While there, he designed book jackets and posters for *Cassell's Magazine*. In 1883 Rhead immigrated to the United States to work as art director at the D. Appleton Company in New York City. After 1891, he visited Paris and was influenced by the designs of French artist Eugène Grasset. Rhead's illustrations echo Grasset's areas of color and broad outlines as well as his emphasis on elegant figures.

Throughout his productive career, Rhead designed at least one hundred posters for magazines, books, and newspapers, and for products such as Lundborg perfumes, Pearline washing powders and cleansers, and Packer's soap. The bold colors of the museum's image are characteristic of American poster art of the late nineteenth century. ▩

Attributed to CHARLES ROHLFS
American, 1853–1936
and CHARLES ROHLFS WORKSHOP
American (Buffalo, New York),
1898–1928

Desk, ca. 1898–1902
Oak, iron, brass
56 x 25 ½ x 23 ¾ in. (142.2 x 64.7 x
60.3 cm)
Gift of Sydney and Frances Lewis, 85.66

Charles Rohlfs was among the most creative artists of the American Arts and Crafts movement. This fall-front desk was inspired by fifteenth-century Gothic furniture. The openwork motifs on the front, however, reflect an awareness of European Art Nouveau. This example displays a number of characteristics that make it unique among similar desks by Rohlfs: it is unsigned by the artist, the carving is slightly different, it has decorative nails, and a swivel is attached to the base. ■

GUSTAV STICKLEY
American, 1858–1942
Made by UNITED CRAFTS
American (Eastwood, New York),
1901–1903
or THE CRAFTSMAN WORKSHOPS
American (Eastwood, New York),
1903–1916

Fall-Front Desk, ca. 1903–4
Oak, copper, pewter, inlaid woods
46 x 42 x 11 ½ in. (116.8 x 106.6 x
29.2 cm)
Marked (back, on paper label): *Cobb
Eastman Co, Boston, Mass.*
Gift of Sydney and Frances Lewis, 85.70

Gustav Stickley was one of the most important leaders of the American Arts
and Crafts movement. Like British theorists John Ruskin and William Morris,
Stickley believed that life could be improved by displaying beautiful objects
in the home. His magazine, *The Craftsman*, promoted such ideals for a
practical American lifestyle. By 1899 he had founded the Gustav Stickley
Company in Eastwood (now Syracuse), New York, and for the next eighteen
years this successful enterprise created architectural plans, furniture, and a
variety of objects for his "Craftsman Houses." Although furniture by Stickley
is often called "Mission Oak" (from the Franciscan missions of California
and Stickley's statement that his furniture fulfilled a "mission of usefulness"),
he used the term "Craftsman Furniture." The inlaid marquetry panels on this
fall-front desk were made by the New York City manufacturer George H.
Jones and purchased by Stickley. ◼

As a theorist and designer, American architect Frank Lloyd Wright had a seminal influence on early twentieth-century decorative arts. After working as chief draftsman for the Chicago architect Louis Sullivan, Wright established his own studio and became well known in the United States and abroad. His work was closely associated with the Arts and Crafts movement and was also strongly influenced by Asian art and architecture. Wright developed a highly personal style, in which every aspect of a project—from the building to the interior decoration, furnishings, and landscape—was related. To this end, he designed furniture, leaded-glass windows, carpets, textiles, and other objects.

In 1899 Wright began building his own house and studio in Oak Park, Illinois, a suburb of Chicago. Serving as both the architect and interior designer, he created this side chair for his own use. The shape and construction relate to furniture by Gustav Stickley and Roycroft and reveal Wright's concern for structural simplicity. The use of geometric shapes and the extension of the back panel below the seat also reflect designs by the Scottish architect Charles Rennie Mackintosh. This chair, like all of Wright's furniture, has a strong relationship to the architecture that he developed during his early years in Chicago. ■

FRANK LLOYD WRIGHT
American, 1867–1959
Made by JOHN W. AYERS COMPANY (?)
American (Chicago, Illinois), 1887–1914

Chair, 1904
Oak, replacement upholstery
40 1/4 x 15 x 18 3/4 in. (102.2 x 38.1 x 47.6 cm)
Gift of the Sydney and Frances Lewis Foundation, 85.74

Darwin Martin, vice president of the Larkin Company soap manufacturers, commissioned Frank Lloyd Wright to design a house and furnishings in Buffalo, New York. The house, constructed between 1903 and 1905, is one of Wright's early architectural masterpieces, and the windows are among the most successful of his career. Inspired by Japanese art, this window from the house consists of three stylized plant forms branching out in a diagonal geometric pattern. The wood frame was made by the Matthews Brothers Furniture Company, active in Milwaukee from 1857 to 1937. ■

FRANK LLOYD WRIGHT
American, 1867–1959
Made by LINDEN GLASS COMPANY
American (Chicago, Illinois),
1890–1934

Window, ca. 1904
Clear glass, iridized glass, cathedral glass,
gilded glass, brass, cypress
47 5/8 x 32 in. (120.5 x 81.3 cm)
Gift of the Sydney and Frances Lewis
Foundation, 85.347

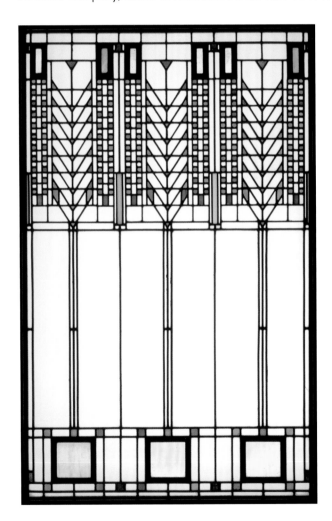

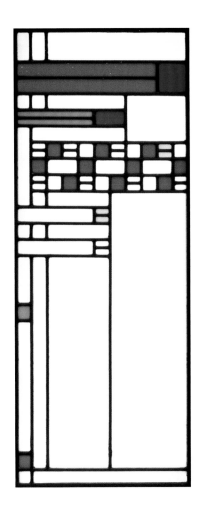
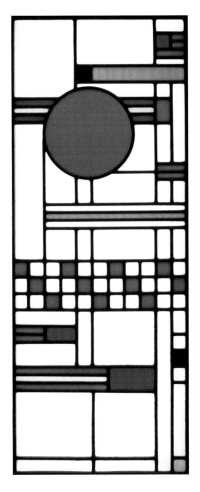

FRANK LLOYD WRIGHT
American, 1867–1959
Made by LINDEN GLASS COMPANY
American (Chicago, Illinois),
1890–1934

Two Windows, 1912
Clear and colored glass, zinc
30 5/8 x 12 1/4 x 3/8 in. (77.8 x 32.1 x .32 cm)
(each)
Gift of Sydney and Frances Lewis,
85.348.1–2

For Frank Lloyd Wright, glass windows and doors served a primary role in architectural decoration. They affected the light and shadow of interiors and created a special environment for the people who inhabited those spaces. These two windows, in bold primary colors, are part of a larger set made for the Avery Coonley Playhouse in Chicago. The bright circles and squares most likely relate to Wright's childhood games using colorful maple blocks and cardboard cutouts of circles and squares. The forms may also have reminded Wright of parades with flags, balloons, and confetti that he enjoyed as a child. ▪

Louis Comfort Tiffany, son of Tiffany and Company cofounder Charles L. Tiffany, was originally trained as a painter, studying first with the landscape artist George Inness. Despite his initial career focus, Tiffany developed his interest in interior decoration and established his own company in 1879. The firm had several names during its lifetime: Louis C. Tiffany and Company, Associated Artists; Tiffany Glass Company; Tiffany Glass and Decorating Company; and finally Tiffany Studios, which continued until 1932.

Through his companies Tiffany offered leaded-glass windows, glass vessels, lamps, mosaics, jewelry, furniture, ceramics, and other objects to consumers. The name Louis Comfort Tiffany is now synonymous with the production of art glass. The term *favrile*, a trade name for Tiffany's glass, is derived from the Latin word *fabrilis* meaning handmade. Tiffany oversaw the production of everything created by artists and craftsman at his firm. One particularly distinguished artist was Clara Driscoll who designed the *Cobweb* and *Wisteria Lamps* in addition to other well-known Tiffany lamps.

Tiffany's triumph at the 1893 Columbian Exposition, in Chicago, established his international reputation, which led to numerous awards. One of the most celebrated pieces of Tiffany's favrile glass created for an international exhibition is the large punch bowl, for which he received both a grand prize and a gold medal at the 1900 Exposition Universelle in Paris. Art dealer Siegfried Bing recognized the importance of Tiffany's glass, and his Parisian art gallery, L'Art Nouveau, became the major distributor for the artist in Europe.

LOUIS COMFORT TIFFANY

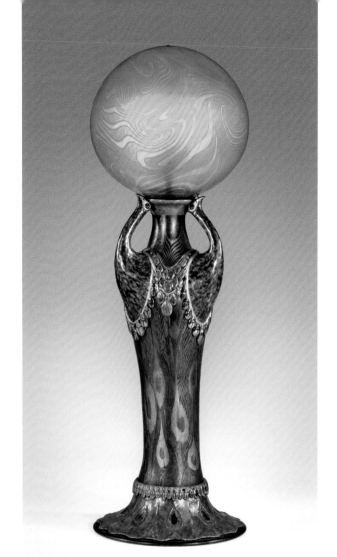

TIFFANY GLASS AND DECORATING COMPANY
American (New York, New York), 1892–1900

Peacock Lamp, ca. 1898–1900
Glass, enamel, brass, gilding
40 ½ x 13 in. (102.9 x 33 cm) diam.
Inscribed (globe, inside rim): *M3460*
Gift of the Sydney and Frances Lewis
Foundation, 85.152a–b

Charles Winthrop Gould, a prominent lawyer, art collector, and trustee of the Metropolitan Museum of Art in New York, commissioned Tiffany to create the interior decoration for his Manhattan house in Washington Square. The peacock, a central design theme of the house, inspired this monumental lamp for Gould. The glass shaft, with a peacock-feather motif, is topped by a glass globe with swirls. This globe is supported by three enameled-brass peacock heads. The foot of the lamp is made of enameled brass with a ring of glass scarabs, echoing those around the birds' necks.

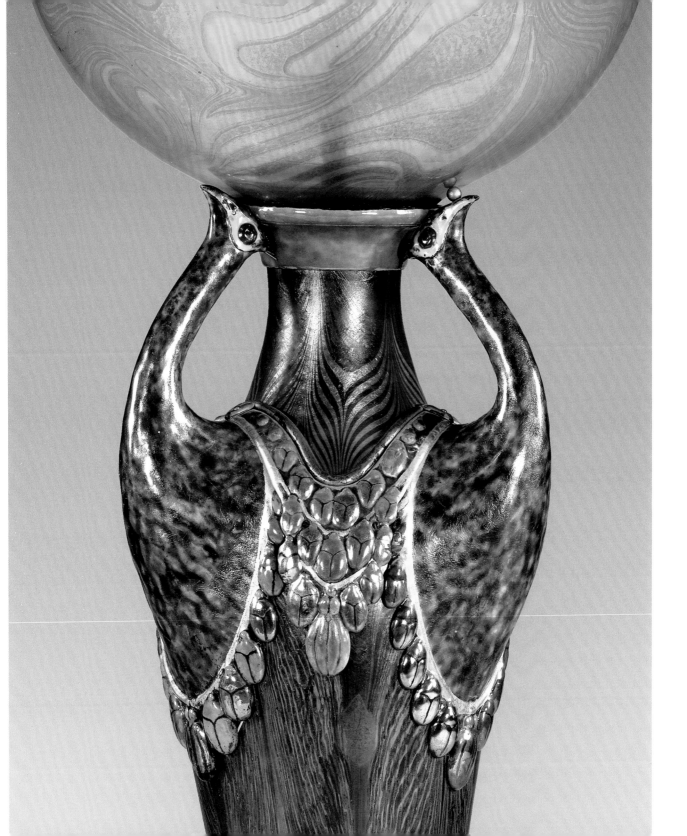

This punch bowl was owned by Henry O. Havemeyer of New York City, one of Louis Comfort Tiffany's distinguished patrons. It is among the most important objects made by the Tiffany Glass and Decorating Company. Formed of Tiffany's handblown favrile glass, the punch bowl's iridescent surface is reminiscent of ancient Roman glass. The gilded-silver mounts are in the form of C and S scrolls in the Art Nouveau style. The bowl was displayed in Tiffany's booth at the 1900 Exposition Universelle in Paris, where the artist won a grand prize and received the French Legion of Honor (fig. 7). It was displayed at the Pan-American Exposition in Buffalo, New York, in 1901.

TIFFANY GLASS AND
DECORATING COMPANY
American (New York, New York),
1892–1900

Punch Bowl with Three Ladles,
1900
Glass, silver, gilding, copper
Bowl: 14 ¼ x 24 in. (36.2 x 60.9 cm)
Ladles (3): 2 ½ x 3 ½ x 10 in. (6.3 x 8.9 x
25.4 cm) (each)
Marked (bowl, bottom): *APRIL 1900 /
TIFFANY G. & D. CO. / New York / 1282*
Sydney and Frances Lewis Art Nouveau
Fund, 74.16

Fig. 7: Louis Comfort Tiffany's booth, Exposition Universelle, Paris, 1900. Virginia Museum of Fine Arts

TIFFANY STUDIOS
American (New York, New York),
1902–1932

Lava Bowl, ca. 1900–1910
Glass
5 3/8 x 7 in. (13.7 x 17.7 cm)
Inscribed (bottom): *L.C. Tiffany Favrile,
22 A-coll.*
Sydney and Frances Lewis Art Nouveau
Fund, 81.195

Tiffany Studios developed a type of handblown glass known as "lava" or "volcanic." Louis Comfort Tiffany's inspiration for the novel invention was likely his trip to Mount Etna, in Sicily, during an active eruption in 1870. According to specialists, the lava glass technique was the most challenging of Tiffany's production. First, a rough black vessel was created by incorporating pieces of basalt or talc into the glass, and then, smooth areas of gold luster were added to the surface. The overall effect suggested hot molten glass flowing from a volcano. The inscription *A-coll.* on the bottom of this bowl indicates that it was originally part of Louis Comfort Tiffany's personal collection. VMFA has several examples of lava glass as well as other types of glass created by the firm, including Cypriote, paperweight, reactive, and aquamarine. ▪

FREDERICK WILSON
Irish (active in America), 1858–1932
Made by TIFFANY GLASS AND
DECORATING COMPANY
American (New York, New York),
1892–1900

Christ Resurrection Window,
ca. 1900
Leaded glass, paint
12 x 12 ft. (3.7 x 3.7 m)
Inscribed (vent, right lancet): *Copyright 1898 /*
Tiffany Glass & Decorating Company /
New York
Gift of All Saints Episcopal Church, Richmond,
Virginia, 2008.48a–c

Fig. 8: All Saints Episcopal Church,
West Franklin Street, Richmond, Virginia.
Photograph courtesy Dementi Studio,
Richmond, Virginia

At the beginning of the twentieth century, leaded-glass windows by the Tiffany Glass and Decorating Company were regularly commissioned by American churches. This window was created for All Saints Episcopal Church in Richmond, Virginia, by Frederick Wilson, who designed thousands of religious figural windows and mosaics for Tiffany. Through experimental glass techniques, the window shows striking effects of color, light, and texture.

The congregation of All Saints Episcopal Church grew out of a Sunday school and evening-services chapel established in 1883 by the city's Monumental Church. In 1887, the congregation began construction on its first Gothic brick church on the east side of Madison Street between Grove Avenue and West Franklin Street. Later, between 1898 and 1900, All Saints Episcopal built a larger church on the north side of the 300 block of West Franklin Street.

This window, installed at the West Franklin Street church (fig. 8) between 1898 and 1901, was commissioned by Mary Jane Ball Saunders as a memorial to her husband, Edmund Archer Saunders, a prominent Richmond merchant. When the congregation moved to its new building on River Road in Henrico County in 1957, the window was placed in storage, where it remained until VMFA acquired it in 2008. The Tiffany Glass and Decorating Company created additional windows for All Saints around 1900. These windows, which are still in place at the River Road location, include *The Beatitudes* in the chapel and *The Te Deum* (now in sections) in the chancel. ▪

I·AM·THE·RESURRECTION·AND
THE·LIFE·SAITH·THE·LORD·HE
THAT·BELIEVETH·IN·ME·THOUGH
HE·WERE·DEAD·YET·SHALL·HE·LIVE
AND·WHOSOEVER·LIVETH·AND·BE
LIEVETH·IN·ME·SHALL·NEVER·DIE
St·JOHN·XI·25·26

IN·MEMORY·OF·EDMUND·ARCHER·SAUNDERS ✝✝·VESTRYMAN·OF·THIS·CHURCH·✝✝ BORN·FEBRUARY·9·1830·DIED·OCTOBER·2·1898

Thousands of carefully selected pieces of glass form the shade of this *Wisteria Lamp*. The top of the leaded-glass and bronze shade is pierced to allow heat from light bulbs to escape. Designed by Clara Driscoll, head of Tiffany's Glass Cutting and Decorating Department, the lamp was created as a luxury object and priced at $400, making it one of the most expensive lamps in the designer's production. Of all those made by the company, it is among the most iconic examples. ▪

CLARA DRISCOLL
American, 1861–1944
Made by TIFFANY GLASS AND
DECORATING COMPANY
American (New York, New York),
1892–1900

Wisteria Lamp, ca. 1901–2
Leaded glass, bronze
27 x 18 ½ in. (68.6 x 47 cm) diam.
Marked (base, bottom): *TGDCo / Tiffany Studios / New York / 26854*;
(base, top): 1; (shade): 1
Gift of Sydney and Frances Lewis,
85.157a–b

CLARA DRISCOLL
American, 1861–1944
Made by TIFFANY GLASS AND
DECORATING COMPANY
American (New York, New York),
1892–1900

Cobweb Lamp, ca. 1902
Leaded glass, bronze, mosaic-glass tiles
29 1/2 x 20 in. (74.9 x 50.9 cm) diam.
Marked (fuel canister, bottom): *TGDCo /
D 658 / Tiffany Studios / New York*
Gift of Sydney and Frances Lewis,
85.164a–b

This lamp is one of several existing cobweb lamps designed by Clara Driscoll, an especially accomplished artist employed by Tiffany. Because of its large size, complex form, octagonal shade, and mosaic-glass tiles, it is one of the most expensive examples created by the Tiffany Glass and Decorating Company. The lamp's intricate construction and complex patterns of cobwebs and flowers showcase the skill of the artists working for Tiffany. The base, formed of bronze branches that rise to support the shade, is decorated with mosaic-glass tiles that depict narcissi. ▪

ART NOUVEAU

Art Nouveau—a term derived from the Paris gallery L'Art Nouveau established by Siegfried Bing in 1895—is a distinct early twentieth-century style in European and American art and architecture. Characterized by an organic quality based on nature and accentuated with variations of the whiplash curve, the Art Nouveau style suggests movement, fantasy, and life. Although the trend was international, its main thrust was in France and Belgium. Working for Bing, the artists Edward Colonna, Georges de Feure, and Eugène Gaillard established the Parisian Art Nouveau style. They also designed interior decoration and objects such as metalwork, textiles, furniture, and ceramics for Bing's Art Nouveau pavilion at the 1900 Exposition Universelle in Paris (fig. 9). Colonna designed a drawing room, which was critically acclaimed at the time (fig. 11). De Feure, a successful artist and interior decorator, and Gaillard, who specialized in furniture and textile design, each created several furnished rooms for Bing's pavilion. The French Art Nouveau collection at VMFA is arguably the finest in an American museum.

Fig. 9: Interior decoration and furnishings designed by Eugène Gaillard for Siegfried Bing's L'Art Nouveau pavilion, Exposition Universelle, Paris, 1900. *L'Art décoratif* (Paris, 1901)

ARTIST UNKNOWN
French, 20th century

Pendant, ca. 1900
Opal, gold, enamel, pearl
4 7/8 x 3 1/8 x 3/4 in. (12.4 x 7.9 x 1.9 cm)
Inscribed (on gold, back): *1 pan d'or 166 ct.*;
(back, lower right): *R*
Gift of Sydney and Frances Lewis, 85.228

This large (166 carats) black fire opal was found in Nevada in the late
nineteenth century and, as indicated by an inscription on the gold,
was mounted in France. Unfortunately, there are no marks that identify
a designer or maker of this sumptuous piece of jewelry. The elaborate
C- and S-shape gold scrolls resemble the whiplash lines associated
with French Art Nouveau. A brooch in a similar style also incorporating
gold decoration was made in the late nineteenth century by the important
French designer and jeweler René Lalique. ■

A talented designer, Félix Aubert created wall decoration, carpets, furnishing fabrics, and lace in the French Art Nouveau style. This textile design incorporates long-stemmed water irises and ribbonlike motifs. Aubert displayed similar furnishing fabrics with water irises at the Exposition Universelle in Paris in 1900. Carefully preserved for decades in the company archives of Scheurer, Lauth et Cie, this textile is in especially good condition. VMFA has two other versions of this fabric in different colors.

FÉLIX AUBERT
French, 1866–1940
Made by SCHEURER, LAUTH ET CIE
French (Alsace, Thann), 1872–1935

Furnishing Fabric, 1897–98
Cotton
30 x 27 in. (76.2 x 68.58 cm)
Swenson Art Nouveau Fund, 2008.32

GEORGES DE FEURE
French, 1868–1943
Made by SCHEURER, LAUTH ET CIE
French (Alsace, Thann), 1872–1935
For L'ART NOUVEAU GALLERY
French (Paris), 1895–1904

Furnishing Fabric, ca. 1900
Cotton velveteen
18 ½ x 32 in. (46.99 x 81.28 cm)
Swenson Art Nouveau Fund, 2008.25

Georges de Feure was a painter, designer, and interior decorator working in Paris around 1900. His designs were executed in metalwork, textiles, carpets, glass, and furniture for a boudoir at Siegfried Bing's pavilion at the Exposition Universelle in Paris in 1900. De Feure's floral textiles in the Art Nouveau style were a big success. This rare panel, identical to those on view at the exposition, features the artist's well-known colors and patterns. It was woven for Bing's Paris gallery, L'Art Nouveau, by Scheurer, Lauth et Cie, in Alsace, France. Carefully preserved for decades in the company's archives, it is in especially good condition. VMFA has six other versions of this textile in different colors. ■

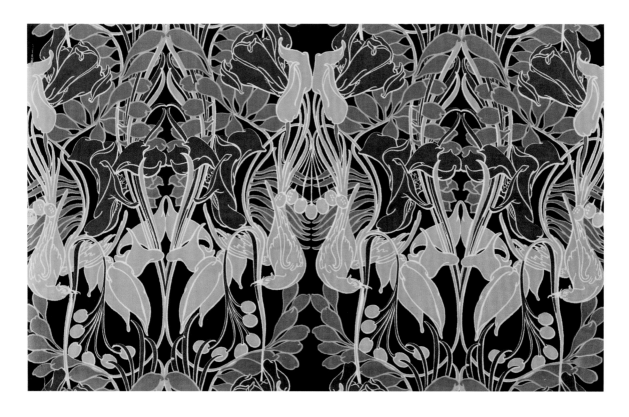

ALPHONSE MUCHA
Czechoslovakian (active in France),
1860–1939
Made by SCHEURER, LAUTH ET CIE
French (Alsace, Thann), 1872–1935

Furnishing Fabric, 1898–1900
Cotton velveteen
27 ⅝ x 30 ¼ in. (70.17 x 76.84 cm)
Swenson Art Nouveau Fund, 2008.36

Alphonse Mucha designed only a few furnishing fabrics with his distinctive
female figures, lush flowers, and foliage; this is a rare example on cotton
velveteen. The pattern was also available in cotton sateen and a heavy-
weight ribbed cotton in a number of colors. Mucha's textiles, which were
used as wall hangings, screens, and pillow covers, were sold in Great
Britain through Hines, Stroud and Company, a London-based printing
firm. Two other versions of this fabric in different colors are also in the
VMFA collection.

Fig. 10: Interior decoration and furnishings designed by Carlo Bugatti for the Snail Room, Prima Esposizione Internazionale d'Arte Decorativa Moderna, Turin, Italy, 1902. *Internationale Ausstellung für moderne dekoration kunst in Turin*, (Germany, 1902)

Following the success of the Exposition Universelle in Paris in 1900, the Italian government organized the Prima Esposizione Internazionale d'Arte Decorativa Moderna (First International Exhibition of Modern Decorative Arts) in Turin in 1902. Carlo Bugatti's interiors and furniture, inspired by Middle Eastern and Asian designs, were considered the most original at the Turin show. Among the three spaces Bugatti designed was a Snail Room (fig. 10), furnished with his distinctive G-profile, or "cobra," chairs in which the seat and back form a continuous curve. These and other pieces he created for Turin are among his most outstanding in both concept and execution; VMFA's chair from the Snail Room is one of the original examples. The museum also has a bench by Bugatti that is the same model as one displayed at the Turin exhibition (fig. 11).

CARLO BUGATTI
Italian, 1855–1940

Chair, ca. 1902
Parchment, wood, copper, paint
35 x 16 ½ x 21 in. (88.9 x 41.8 x 58.3 cm)
Sydney and Frances Lewis Art Nouveau Fund, 72.10

Fig. 11: **Bench,** ca. 1902, Carlo Bugatti, wood, parchment, copper, brass, paint, leather, 36 ⅜ x 35 ½ x 16 ¾ in. (92.3 x 90.2 x 42.5 cm). Gift of Lloyd and Barbara Macklowe, 89.141

SARAH BERNHARDT
French, 1844–1923
Cast by THIÉBAUT FRÈRES
French (Paris), 1844–1926

Inkwell (Self-Portrait as Sphinx),
1880
Bronze
12 x 13 ⅜ x 12 ⅝ in. (30.5 x 34 x 32 cm)
Inscribed (base, left): *Sarah Bernhardt / 1880*
Marked (base, back): *Thiébaut Frères Fondeurs Paris*
Gift of the Fabergé Society of the Virginia Museum of Fine Arts, 99.24a–b

Celebrated throughout Europe and the United States, stage actress Sarah Bernhardt thrilled audiences with her dramatic voice as well as her equally theatrical lifestyle. She commissioned Alphonse Mucha to create numerous colorful posters of her in various stage productions. Around 1869 Bernhardt herself began creating paintings and sculpture. She displayed several portraits at the Paris Salon of 1875.

A bronze inkwell like this example was probably on view at Bernhardt's first exhibition of paintings and sculpture in London in 1879. A year later, a similar version was displayed at the Union League Club of New York in a show titled *Sarah Bernhardt Souvenir, including the Authorised Catalogue of her Paintings and Sculptures.* The masks representing comedy and tragedy on either arm of this sculpture may be an allusion to Bernhardt's acting career.

FRANÇOIS-RUPERT CARABIN
French, 1862–1932

Fountain and Bowl, 1897–98
Walnut, stoneware, pewter
70 ¼ x 34 ⅞ x 12 ¾ in. (178.4 x 88.6 x 32.4 cm)
Inscribed (water container, lower right): *R. Carabin 10*
Gift of Sydney and Frances Lewis, 85.94

François-Rupert Carabin, sculptor, wood-carver, and draftsman,
worked in a variety of materials including clay, wood, wax, bronze,
precious metals, and ceramics. A series of his bronze figures depicting the American dancer Loïe Fuller is part of the VMFA collection.
Carabin often created female nudes in both his sculpture and carved-
wood furniture. Here, the stoneware figure is a container for water,
and the ceramic pond and lily pads below serve as the catch basin
and soap dishes. The wood bracket at the upper right is a towel rack.
An almost identical fountain and bowl, now at the Musée d'Orsay
in Paris, was displayed at the Salon of the Société Nationale des
Beaux-Arts (National Society of Fine Arts) in Paris in 1898. ■

EDWARD COLONNA
German (active in France), 1862–1948
Made by WORKSHOP OF L'ART
NOUVEAU
French (Paris), 1898–1904
For L'ART NOUVEAU GALLERY
French (Paris), 1895–1904

Settee and Armchair, ca. 1899
Maple, replacement fabric
Settee: 39 ¼ x 44 ¾ x 21 in. (99.7 x
113.6 x 53.5 cm)
Armchair: 38 ⅜ x 24 x 21 in. (98.4 x 61 x
53.5 cm)
Gift of Sydney and Frances Lewis, 85.139.1–2

Edward Colonna, designer of furniture, jewelry, ceramics, and textiles, worked in France in the early 1890s, creating his most important pieces in the Art Nouveau style. From 1898 to 1903 he was associated with Siegfried Bing and his L'Art Nouveau gallery in Paris. This settee and armchair, which retailed at Bing's gallery, are similar to examples displayed in Bing's pavilion at the Exposition Universelle in Paris in 1900 (fig. 12). VMFA also has a set of gilded-silver spoons designed by Colonna that are joined with six glass salts by Louis Comfort Tiffany, all of which are fitted in a silk box. The spoons and box were made in Bing's workshops, and the entire set was displayed at his pavilion at the Exposition Universelle. ■

EDWARD COLONNA
German (active in France), 1862–1948
Made by GÉRARD, DUFRAISSEX
ET ABBOT
French (Limoges), founded 1900
For L'ART NOUVEAU GALLERY
French (Paris), 1895–1904

Pair of Vases or Lamp Bases,
ca. 1901–3

Hard-paste porcelain, enamel

12 ½ x 4 ¼ in. (32.7 x 10.8 cm) (each)
Marked (bottom): artist's monogram;
monogram for L'Art Nouveau Bing /
LEUCONOÉ / 512
Gift of Lloyd and Barbara Macklowe,
90.218.1–2

VMFA has several porcelain objects that were commissioned by Siegfried Bing for his Parisian gallery L'Art Nouveau. The well-known establishment sold British and European furniture, ceramics, metalwork, glass, and other art objects. Bing and several of his in-house designers, such as Edward Colonna and Georges de Feure, collaborated with Gérard, Dufraissex et Abbot to make objects for sale in his gallery. The porcelain that Bing ordered is representative of Paris Art Nouveau. These pieces are generally marked with the artist's monogram as well as the name of Bing's gallery. This porcelain was regularly displayed at the salons of the Société Nationale des Beaux-Arts in Paris, including a pair like VMFA's vases in 1902.

Fig. 12: Interior decoration and furnishings designed by Edward Colonna for Siegfried Bing's pavilion, Exposition Universelle, Paris, 1900. *The Studio* (London, 1900)

ADRIEN DELOVINCOURT
French, dates unknown
Made by GÉRARD, DUFRAISSEX
ET ABBOT
French (Limoges), founded 1900
For L'ART NOUVEAU GALLERY
French (Paris), 1895–1904

Bonbonniere, ca. 1900–1902
Hard-paste porcelain
4 x 6 in. (10.2 x 15.3 cm)
Marked (bottom): monogram for L'Art
Nouveau Bing; (bottom, on paper label):
E. 149; A LA PAIX / 34; Ave de l'Opera; PARIS
Gift of Lloyd and Barbara Macklowe,
90.214a–b

A bonbonniere is a small box or
dish for storing bonbons or other
candies. ▪

GEORGES DE FEURE
French, 1868–1943
Made by GÉRARD, DUFRAISSEX
ET ABBOT
French (Limoges), founded 1900
For L'ART NOUVEAU GALLERY
French (Paris), 1895–1904

Lidded Jar, ca. 1901–3
Hard-paste porcelain, enamel
5 x 3 ½ in. (12.7 x 8.9 cm)
Marked (bottom): artist's monogram;
monogram for L'Art Nouveau Bing /
LEUCONOÉ
Gift of Lloyd and Barbara Macklowe,
90.215a–b

A similar jar was displayed at the
Salon of the Société Nationale des
Beaux-Arts in Paris in 1901. ▪

GEORGES DE FEURE
French, 1868–1943
Made by GÉRARD, DUFRAISSEX
ET ABBOT
French (Limoges), founded 1900
For L'ART NOUVEAU GALLERY
French (Paris), 1895–1904

Vase, ca. 1901–3
Hard-paste porcelain
11 ⅞ x 4 in. (30.2 x 10.2 cm)
Marked (bottom): artist's monogram;
monogram for L'Art Nouveau Bing /
LEUCONOÉ / 500
Gift of Lloyd and Barbara Macklowe, 90.216

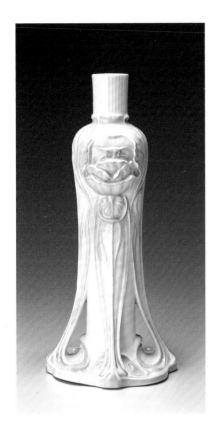

GEORGES DE FEURE
French, 1868–1943
Made by GÉRARD, DUFRAISSEX
ET ABBOT
French (Limoges), founded 1900
For L'ART NOUVEAU GALLERY
French (Paris), 1895–1904

Lamp Base, ca. 1901–3
Hard-paste porcelain, enamel
13 5/8 x 6 1/4 in. (34.6 x 15.8 cm)
Marked (bottom): artist's monogram;
monogram for L'Art Nouveau Bing /
LEUCONOÉ / 522
Gift of Lloyd and Barbara Macklowe, 90.217

GEORGES DE FEURE
French, 1868–1943
Made by GÉRARD, DUFRAISSEX
ET ABBOT
French (Limoges), founded 1900
For L'ART NOUVEAU GALLERY
French (Paris), 1895–1904

Lidded Box, ca. 1900–1901
Hard-paste porcelain, enamel
Box: 2 1/4 x 7 x 7 in. (5.7 x 17.8 x 17.8 cm)
Lid: 2 1/2 x 7 1/2 x 7 1/2 in. (6.4 x 19 x 19 cm)
Marked (bottom): artist's monogram;
monogram for L'Art Nouveau Bing /
LEUCONOÉ

Sydney and Frances Lewis Art Nouveau
Fund, 77.48a–b

A similar box was displayed at
the Salon of the Société Nationale
des Beaux-Arts in Paris in 1902
and, in the same year, at the
Prima Esposizione Internazionale
d'Arte Decorativa Moderna in
Turin, Italy. ▪

GEORGES DE FEURE
French, 1868–1943

Project for a Tapestry, 1895–96
Oil on canvas
45 ½ x 37 ½ in. (115 x 95 cm)
Inscribed (bottom left): *G. van Feure 95*
Original Frame by Georges de Feure
Wood, paint
Inscribed (back): *15, rue Bréda* [Paris]
Sydney and Frances Lewis Endowment Fund,
2013.173

Georges de Feure, who regularly exhibited his paintings in the "Objects of Art" section at the Salon of the Société Nationale des Beaux-Arts in Paris, presented this model for the tapetry known as *The Fairy Caprice* there in 1896. De Feure was a versatile artist who designed many objects— stained glass, furniture, ceramics, metalwork, textiles, illustrations for books, and posters—in the Art Nouveau style. This impressive decorative painting has been interpreted as a medieval-like transcription of the legend of Perseus, who slayed Medusa and presented the head to Minerva, goddess of wisdom.

Like other artists active in the late nineteenth century—for example, Paul Ranson and Alphonse Mucha—de Feure created designs in oil, watercolor, and pencil for tapestries, textiles, and all manner of decorative arts. Though it is not known if a tapestry was ever made from this painting, de Feure apparently often worked out his design ideas in preliminary oil paintings such as this canvas—among his most elaborate productions. It is also one of the only known examples to include an ornamental wood frame, painted by the artist and intrinsic to the work's overall significance and visual impact. ■

GEORGES DE FEURE
French, 1868–1943
Made by HANS MÜLLER-HICKLER (?)
German (active in Darmstadt),
1860–1933
For L'ART NOUVEAU GALLERY
French (Paris), 1895–1904

Window, ca. 1901–2
Stained and leaded glass
78 ¾ x 35 ¹³⁄₁₆ in. (200 x 90.9 cm)
Gift of Sydney and Frances Lewis, 85.349

In the late nineteenth century, Georges de Feure designed several leaded-glass windows depicting women for Siegfried Bing's L'Art Nouveau pavilion at the 1900 Exposition Universelle in Paris. In addition, the artist created large paintings of women for the exterior of the pavilion, and for the interior, he designed various pieces of furniture, metalwork, textiles, and ceramics.

VMFA's leaded-glass window designed by de Feure, which was probably made by Hans Müller-Hickler, shows a woman surrounded by floral imagery. It relates to the windows de Feure created for the Paris 1900 exposition. Commissioned by Bing for his Parisian gallery L'Art Nouveau, this window was most likely also shown at the de Feure exhibition held at the art dealer's establishment in 1903. It is among the most spectacular examples of French Art Nouveau stained glass in the United States. After ending his employment with Bing, de Feure worked on his own as an artist and interior designer. ▪

GEORGES FOUQUET
French, 1862–1957

Brooch, 1904
Gold, enamel, opal, ivory-colored stone,
glass, diamonds, pearls
3 ¾ x 7 ¾ x ½ in. (9.5 x 19.6 x 1.27 cm)
Inscribed (back, top left wing): *G. Fouquet
5473*
Gift of Sydney and Frances Lewis, 85.242

In 1860, Alphonse Fouquet started his jewelry firm in Paris with about thirty workers. His son Georges joined the company in 1880 and assumed leadership in 1895. Georges Fouquet's jewelry in the Art Nouveau style, made in collaboration with the artist and designer Alphonse Mucha, was displayed at the 1900 Exposition Universelle in Paris, where he received international acclaim. Fouquet's jewelry is often compared to the Art Nouveau designs of René Lalique. After the First World War, the Fouquet firm was one of the leading jewelers in Paris. With the 1929 stock market crash, however, the distinguished company suffered financial losses and closed in 1936.

This 1904 brooch, known as an *ornement de corsage* (adornment for the bodice), includes a woman's face and shoulders carved in ivory-colored stone; her locks of hair are formed of gold. The gold halo above her head is set with an opal, and the four fan-shape flower forms are made of enamel and glass. Flanking the woman's face are wings of enamel with diamonds set in gold. A baroque pearl hangs at the bottom of the brooch. VMFA also has the brooch's original box, which is inscribed with Fouquet's Paris address, *6, rue Royale.* ▪

ÉMILE GALLÉ
French, 1846–1904

Ladle, ca. 1900
Glass; marquetry, acid etched, engraved,
and internally decorated
5 ¾ x 10 x 4 in. (14.6 x 25.4 x 10.2 cm)
Inscribed (front, right): *Gallé*
Sydney and Frances Lewis Art Nouveau
Fund, 75.6

During the late 1880s, glass by Émile Gallé was celebrated throughout
the world, winning many prizes at major international exhibitions. By
1900, Gallé employed more than three hundred people in his workshops.
The carved decoration on the interior of the ladle shows Gallé's interest
in forms based on nature and his expertise in glass marquetry to create
sculptural effects. The process involved adding various glass fragments
onto the hot glass body of a vessel. Here, seashell-shaped forms are set
into the ladle, creating a textural, three-dimensional surface.

ÉMILE GALLÉ
French, 1846–1904

Sideboard, 1903
Walnut, oak, chestnut, fruitwoods, iron,
gilding, glass
107 x 83 x 27 ½ in. (271.7 x 210.8 x
69.9 cm)
Inscribed (left side): *Salon des Beaux-Arts –
1903;* (door, left): *Gallé*
Sydney and Frances Lewis Art Nouveau
Fund, 77.4

Fig. 13: Furniture designed by Émile Gallé
for the Salon of the Société Nationale des
Beaux-Arts in Paris, 1903. Courtesy Reunion
des musées nationaux

The French city of Nancy is about 120 miles east of Paris in the province of Lorraine. Since the late sixteenth century, Nancy had been a center of the glass-making industry, and in the mid-to-late nineteenth century, several glass factories were still active in the region. One was owned by Charles Gallé, whose son Émile—among the most important French Art Nouveau artists— became the leader of a group known as L'Alliance Provinciale des Industries d'Art, or École de Nancy (School of Nancy), incorporated in 1901. The circle also included such remarkable designers as August and Antonin Daum, Jacques Gruber, Louis Majorelle, Victor Prouvé, and Eugène Vallin. Members were inspired by the forms of nature and incorporated them into their furniture, glass, and ceramics. One of the most successful Nancy designers was Jacques Gruber, known for both his sculptural furniture and his stained-glass windows. Louis Majorelle, considered one of the foremost furniture manufacturers in France, decorated his nature-inspired pieces with stylized lilies of gilded bronze.

Émile Gallé is best known for his glass, ceramics, and furniture in the French Art Nouveau style. Like this sideboard, which includes elements inspired by autumn, his furniture is usually thematic. Harvest scenes decorate the panels on the lower doors, gilded-iron wheat sheaves form the drawer pulls, and carved-wood wheat sheaves flank the top half of the cabinet. The large gilded-iron snowflakes and twisted stems at the center suggest the coming of winter. Paul Holderbach, who was in charge of Gallé's sculpture studio, created the gilded-iron mounts, and August Herbst designed the marquetry panels. This sideboard was displayed at the Salon of the Société Nationale des Beaux-Arts in Paris in 1903 (fig. 13). ▪

Designed by EUGÈNE GRASSET
Swiss (active in Paris), 1845–1917
Made by MAISON VEVER
French (Paris), 1821–1982

The Sorcerers Necklace, 1900
Gold, enamel, carnelian, chrysoprase
Marked (on reverse): E. GRASSET del. 1900;
VEVER PARIS
5 ½ in. (14.7 cm) (pendant)
17 in. (44.5 cm) (chain)
Sydney and Frances Lewis Endowment Fund,
2014.167

Maison Vever was a distinguished jewelry firm in Paris during the nineteenth and twentieth centuries. Pierre Paul Vever set up the business in 1821. After serving a long apprenticeship, his son Ernest took over operations in 1848. In 1874 Ernest's sons Paul and Henri became their father's partners. Paul assisted Ernest with the administrative and commercial aspects of the company, while Henri dealt with artistic matters. Beginning in 1889, natural themes predominated in their innovative designs. This style gained popularity and triumphed around 1900 as "Art Nouveau," in which the principal subjects of flora and fauna were linked with the female form.

The highly creative objects presented by Maison Vever at the 1900 Exposition Universelle in Paris were impressive in both number and quality. The display featured jewelry that represented the firm as well as a selection of twenty objects, including this necklace, designed by Eugène Grasset. Jewelry by Grasset, which incorporated mythical female forms, animals, and flowers (fig. 14), was described at the time as "painters' jewels," for their appearance was achieved as if by brushstroke with enamels or gold. Maison Vever was awarded the prestigious Grand Prize for its display, a rich testimony to Art Nouveau jewelry and to the company's success in combining tradition with this new "artistic" style. This necklace by Grasset depicts two sorcerers, recognized as such by their threatening grimaces. Charles Gillot, a printer for whom Grasset provided many book illustrations, acquired it for his wife, Marie.

Fig. 14: *Design for a Brooch*, ca. 1900, Eugène Grasset, gouache and watercolor over pencil underdrawing, 12 ⅝ x 9 ⅞ in. (32 x 25 cm). John and Maria Shugars Fund, 2013.6. The brooch itself was displayed at the Exposition Universelle in Paris in 1900.

JACQUES GRUBER
French, 1870–1936

Window, ca. 1912
Stained and leaded glass
59 ½ x 52 ½ in. (151 x 133.3 cm)
Inscribed (front, lower left): *Jacques Gruber Nancy*
Sydney and Frances Lewis Art Nouveau Fund, 75.26

A prominent member of the School of Nancy, Jacques Gruber was a major designer, cabinetmaker, and stained-glass artist. He studied at the École des Beaux-Arts (School of Fine Arts) in Nancy and later at the École Nationale des Arts Décoratifs (National School of Decorative Arts) in Paris. One of his teachers was the well-known artist Gustave Moreau. In 1893 Gruber returned to Nancy and taught decorative composition at the École des Beaux-Arts. He also designed and decorated glass for the Daum Frères manufactory. In 1897 Gruber founded his own workshop where he created stained-glass windows for both private residences and public buildings.

This window is primarily triple layered and features "bubbles" of molded opalescent glass. The water lilies are acid-etched cameo glass, and the rippled surface of the hanging leaves lends definition to the plant forms. There are additional layers of colored glass on the reverse side. The window was displayed at the Salon of the Société Nationale des Beaux-Arts in Paris in 1912. ■

JACQUES GRUBER
French, 1870–1936

Desk and Chair, ca. 1900
Mahogany, bronze, gilding, replacement
upholstery
Desk: 37 ½ x 56 ¾ x 33 in. (94.5 x 144.1 x
83.8 cm)
Chair: 31 ¼ x 30 ½ x 25 in. (79.3 x 77.5 x
63.5 cm)
Inscribed (desk, top right): *Gruber Nancy*
Gift of Sydney and Frances Lewis,
85.86.1–2

Evidence of Jacques Gruber's skill at faithful re-creations of nature, this desk and chair appear to rise gracefully from the earth. The desk relates to a similar example displayed at the Salon of Nancy in 1901. Gruber, who also designed furniture for decorator Louis Majorelle, did not have a cabinetmaking shop, so he employed furniture makers in Nancy, including Justin Férez, Georges-Léon Schwartz, and Laurent Neiss, to execute his designs. ▪

Hector Guimard was one of the most talented architects and designers in Europe during the early twentieth century. Born in Lyon, France, he studied at the École Nationale des Arts Décoratifs and the École des Beaux-Arts in Paris. Guimard created total environments, from a building's basic architecture to every aspect of its interior, such as furniture, metalwork, and textiles. He also designed the city's well-known Metro stations. Representing the highest quality in cabinetmaking, this office suite made for Guimard's own house on the avenue Mozart in Paris displays the architect's use of botanical motifs based on plant stems and roots. The carved decoration in high relief unifies the suite.

(Overleaf)

HECTOR GUIMARD
French, 1867–1942
Made by GUIMARD'S ATELIERS D'ART
ET DE FABRICATION
French (Paris), 1897–1914

Office Suite, 1909
Pear wood, mahogany, bronze, glass,
leather, replacement fabric
Desk, file cabinets (2); armchair, chairs (2)
Desk: 38 x 75 ⅜ x 27 ¾ in. (96.5 x
191.4 x 70.5 cm)
File cabinets: 75 ¼ x 30 ¾ x 14 ⅞ in.
(191.1 x 78.1 x 37.8 cm) (each)
Armchair: 35 x 26 ¼ x 20 in. (88.9 x
66.6 x 52 cm)
Chairs: 33 x 17 ¼ x 20 ½ in. (83.8 x
43.8 x 52 cm) (each)
Inscribed (each piece): *Hector Guimard
1909*
Gift of Sydney and Frances Lewis,
85.87.1–6

HECTOR GUIMARD
French, 1867–1942
Made by GUIMARD'S ATELIERS
D'ART ET DE FABRICATION
French (Paris), 1897–1914

Cabinet, ca. 1897–99 (remodeled
after 1909)
Pear, ash, bronze, mirrored glass, glass
117 x 93 ½ x 19 ½ in. (297.2 x 237.5 x
49.5 cm)
Sydney and Frances Lewis Art Nouveau
Fund, 72.12

This monumental cabinet, with its twisting lines and hollow spaces inspired by nature, was made for Hector Guimard's own office in the Castel Béranger, a Paris apartment building erected between 1894 and 1898 that he designed in the Art Nouveau style. Judging from the original drawings (now at the Musée d'Orsay) for this cabinet, Guimard initially planned an even more elaborate piece of furniture. Sometime after 1909, when he transferred his office and its furnishings from the Castel Béranger to his newly constructed house on the avenue Mozart in Paris, this cabinet was remodeled. Guimard conceived it as part of the overall interior design, not as a separate piece of furniture. VMFA has other objects designed by Guimard, including ceramics, stained glass, and metalwork, as well as a portfolio of prints of his plans for the Castel Béranger apartment building. ▪

Victor Horta is considered to be the father of Art Nouveau architecture. In 1893 he designed one of the earliest houses in that style, a residence in Brussels for Emile Tassel, who granted the architect complete artistic freedom. Once Horta had made a name for himself, Armand Solvay commissioned him to build another house in Brussels, for which this desk was specifically made. Solvay also allowed Horta free artistic rein and unlimited financing to complete the interior decoration and furnishings for his house. The curvilinear edges of the desktop are repeated in the multicolored-marble insert that served as the writing surface. This desk is one of the very few examples of Horta's furniture in the United States.

VICTOR HORTA
Belgian, 1861–1947

Desk, ca. 1897–1903
Belgian ash, marble, bronze, gilding
30 x 55 x 43 in. (76.2 x 139.7 x 109.2 cm)
Gift of the Sydney and Frances Lewis
Foundation, 2005.72

Although known today mainly as a glassmaker, René Lalique was the most important French jeweler working in the Art Nouveau style. Like other artists in the late nineteenth century, Lalique was inspired by nature in his designs. In the mid-1880s, he opened his own jewelry shop, attracting such well-known clients as French stage actress Sarah Bernhardt. One of Lalique's triumphs was his jewelry display at the Exposition Universelle in Paris in 1900.

RENÉ LALIQUE
French, 1860–1945

Sabbath Princess Collar, ca.1899
Gold, enamel, glass, pearls
2 3/16 x 12 x 1/8 in. (5.7 x 30.5 x 4 cm)
Inscribed (front, top edge of frog's eye):
LALIQUE
Gift of Sydney and Frances Lewis, 85.243

Lalique regularly incorporated glass, enamels, and semiprecious stones in his jewelry. He believed that the artistic value of jewelry should be reflected in the design rather than in the cost of precious stones. This unique collar, which features a central enamel panel depicting a female profile surrounded by numerous frogs, is based on *The Sabbath Princess*. The two-act ballet, choreographed by Louis Ganne to a libretto by Jean Lorrain, had opened in Paris in January 1899. A description of this collar was published in an article by Pol Neveux in *Art et Décoration* (1900), proof that it was on display in Lalique's booth at the Exposition Universelle in Paris in 1900. ▪

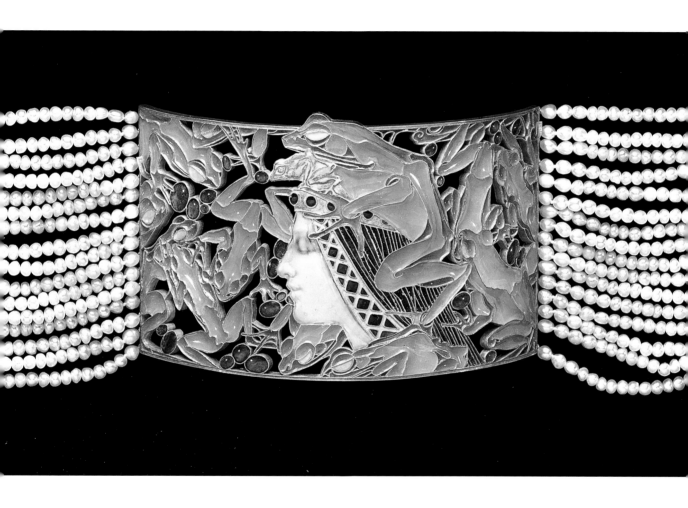

René Lalique's *Sea Horses Brooch* is decorated in delicate enamel and gold with a large opal at the top and an irregularly shaped pearl hanging below. This masterpiece features plique-á-jour enamel—thin glass that allows light to shine through. VMFA has other rare examples of Art Nouveau jewelry by Lalique, including three brooches, a buckle, a collar, a diadem, and a necklace. ■

RENÉ LALIQUE
French, 1860–1945

Sea Horses Brooch, ca. 1902–5
Gold, opals, oriental pearl, enamel
4 x 2 ½ x ½ in. (10.2 x 6.3 x 1.27 cm)
Inscribed (back, top edge): *LALIQUE*
Sydney and Frances Lewis Art Nouveau
Fund, 73.46.1

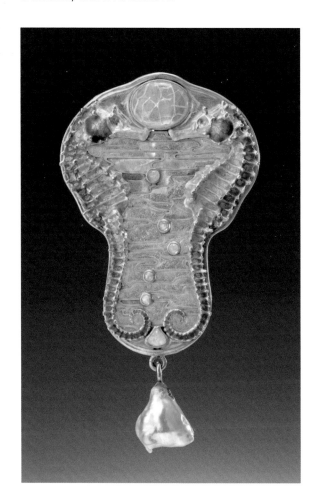

RAOUL FRANÇOIS LARCHE
French, 1860–1912
Cast by SIOT-DECAUVILLE
French (Paris), 1881–1926

Loïe Fuller Lamp, ca. 1900
Bronze, gilding
18 x 8 x 10 in. (45.7 x 20.2 x 25.4 cm)
Inscribed (bottom): *RAOUL LARCHE*
Marked: *Siot Decauville Fondeur Paris*
Sydney and Frances Lewis Art Nouveau
Fund, 72.5.1

Fig. 15: Loïs Fuller, silver gelatin photograph,
ca. 1890s. Musée d'Orsay, Paris

The American dancer Mary Louise Fuller (fig. 15), of Fullersburg, Illinois, became an instant success after performing as Loïe Fuller at the Folies-Bergère in Paris in November 1892. An early innovator in stage lighting, she incorporated long, flowing veils in her dances and was the inspiration for many artists of the period, including sculptor Raoul François Larche.

Larche was awarded a gold medal for his work at the 1900 Exposition Universelle in Paris, where he displayed an example of this lamp, one of four variations. Loïe Fuller, who died in 1926, is still a recognized symbol of French Art Nouveau. VMFA has another, earlier variation of this lamp, dated to about 1896, as well as a bronze sculpture by Pierre Roche that depicts the dancer. ▪

Louis Majorelle was a prominent manufacturer of furniture in the Art Nouveau style. Majorelle's triumph was his display at the Exposition Universelle in Paris in 1900. By 1910 he had opened galleries to sell his furniture, lighting fixtures, and objects of art in Nancy, Paris, Lyon, and Lille.

This buffet is decorated with marquetry characteristic of Majorelle's furniture of the late nineteenth century. The openwork sides at the top are veneered with maple and cut to resemble snails; figures of rabbits and cattails appear in the back marquetry. In all, the marquetry comprises at least eight different woods. The undecorated surfaces are veneered in palisander, a type of Brazilian rosewood. The drawer pulls are cast in the form of ducks' heads holding snakes in their bills.

LOUIS MAJORELLE
French, 1859–1926

Buffet, ca. 1898
Oak, ebony, maple, chestnut, palisander, various woods, bronze, gilding
57 x 52 x 20 ½ in. (144.8 x 132 x 52 cm)
Inscribed (door, lower right): *L. Majorelle*
Sydney and Frances Lewis Art Nouveau Fund, 73.46.2

This bedroom suite represents a high point in Louis Majorelle's career. Designed and executed with remarkable skill, it shows the craftsmanship for which Majorelle's firm was widely known. The organic lines of the design are derived from floral forms generally associated with Art Nouveau. In 1899 Majorelle began to use gilded-bronze mounts in the shape of water lilies as decorative motifs on his furniture; by 1900, the Majorelle firm had a studio for metalwork to make drawer pulls and mounts. This suite is a masterpiece, owing to the fine woods; soft, undulating curves; gilded-bronze mounts and pulls; and marquetry panels in abstract patterns. It is probably one of the most important examples of French Art Nouveau furniture in the United States. The July 1909 issue of *Art et Industrie* published two photographs of this suite. Another version of VMFA's bed is at the Musée d'Orsay in Paris, while a third example is in a private collection.

(Overleaf)

LOUIS MAJORELLE
French, 1859–1926

Bedroom Suite, ca. 1905–8
Mahogany, rosewood, marquetry of woods, bronze, gilding, replacement fabric
Bed, nightstands (2), armoire, armchairs (2), chairs (2)
Bed: 79 x 80 ½ x 90 in. (200.6 x 204 x 228.6 cm)
Armoire: 88 x 96 x 31 in. (23.5 x 243.8 x 78.7 cm)
Armchairs: 44 ½ x 26 ¼ x 25 ¼ in. (113 x 66.6 x 64.1 cm) (each)
Chairs: 39 ½ x 16 ¼ x 18 ½ in. (100.3 x 41.5 x 47 cm) (each)
Nightstands: 47 x 22 x 17 ½ in. (119.3 x 55.8 x 44.5 cm) (each)
Gift of Sydney and Frances Lewis, 85.90.1–8

ALPHONSE MUCHA
Czechoslovakian (active in France),
1860–1939
Printed by F. CHAMPENOIS
French (Paris), active 1875–1915

Carnation, Lily, Iris, and **Rose**
(from the series **Les Fleurs**), 1898
Lithograph on silk
41 x 17 in. (104.1 x 43.1 cm) (each)
Inscribed (each panel): *Mucha*
Sydney and Frances Lewis Art Nouveau
Fund, 73.11.1–4

Alphonse Mucha was a leading Art Nouveau artist in late nineteenth-century Paris. He is best known for his posters depicting sensual women with flowing hair. His subjects included the celebrated stage actress Sarah Bernhardt, with whom he worked in the mid-1890s. An exceptionally skilled designer, Mucha created numerous advertisements—for cigarette paper, champagne, and railroads—as well as magazine and book illustrations. His printed designs of jewelry, metalwork, ornamental motifs, and textile patterns from a portfolio titled *Documents Décoratifs* (1902) are part of the VMFA collection.

Like other Art Nouveau artists, Mucha was especially inspired by nature, which is evident in his lavish use of flowers and foliage. The watercolor panels for *Carnation* and *Iris*, in the *Les Fleurs* series, were initially displayed at Mucha's *Salon des Cent* exhibition, which opened in Paris in June 1897, but the entire series only became available as a set to the public in 1898. These lithographs are among the most successful panels created by Mucha. The printer Champenois issued a deluxe edition on satin, which sold for 100 francs a set. The series was also published as small postcards.

ALPHONSE MUCHA
Czechoslovakian (active in France),
1860–1939
Cast by ÉMILE PINÉDO (?)
French, 1840–1916

Nature, ca. 1900
Bronze, silver, gilding, marble
27 ¼ x 11 x 12 in. (69.2 x 27.9 x 30.5 cm)
Inscribed (right): *Mucha*
Marked (left): *Bronze Garanti Au Titre PARIS*
Sydney and Frances Lewis Art Nouveau
Fund, 72.13

Around 1899 Alphonse Mucha developed the concept of this female portrait bust representing Nature, which is now recognized as one of his most important sculptures. He displayed a cast of the bust in the Austrian section of the Exposition Universelle in Paris in 1900. VMFA's example, most likely cast by Émile Pinédo, is one of about six versions known to exist. The figure's swirling locks of hair show Mucha's skill in creating dynamic movement in a static medium. The artist thought so highly of this model that he also showed an example at the Prima Esposizione Internazionale d'Arte Decorativa Moderna in Turin in 1902. ■

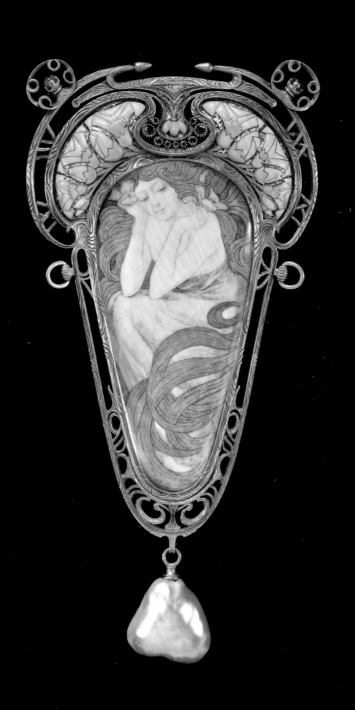

ALPHONSE MUCHA
Czechoslovakian (active in France),
1860–1939
Made by GEORGES FOUQUET
French, 1862–1957

Bodice Adornment, ca. 1900
Gold, enamel, emeralds, pearl,
mother-of-pearl, watercolor, metallic paint
6 $^{11}/_{16}$ x 3 $^3/_8$ x $^9/_{32}$ in. (17 x 8.6 x .7 cm)
Marked (back): *G FOUQUET 2873*
Gift of Sydney and Frances Lewis, 85.253

Among the jewelry that Georges Fouquet displayed at the Exposition Universelle in Paris in 1900 were several critically acclaimed bodice ornaments. One of these was nearly identical to this VMFA example designed by Alphonse Mucha for Fouquet. Mucha also designed other spectacular jewelry for Fouquet as well as the exterior and interior of the jeweler's shop on the rue Royale in Paris. VMFA has several other pieces of Art Nouveau jewelry by Fouquet.

PIEL FRÈRES
French (Paris), 1855–1925

Belt, 1899–1900
Silver, enamel, gilding
9 in. (22.86 cm)
Swenson Art Nouveau Fund, 2010.89

In 2002, VMFA acquired from Karl and Gisela Kreuzer of Munich, Germany, an important collection of approximately five hundred buckles and related necklaces, belts, and buttons dating from about 1890 to 1910. The Kreuzer Collection has many Arts and Crafts and Art Nouveau buckles from Germany, France, Austria, Bohemia, Great Britain, Russia, Scandinavia, and the United States. The handcrafted belt buckles as well as machine-made objects were produced by many of the major designers and

Fig. 16: Women wearing buckles, ca. 1900. Virginia Museum of Fine Arts

manufacturers. Well-known artists, including Josef Hoffmann, Patriz Huber, Georg Jensen, Archibald Knox, René Lalique, and Henry van de Velde, created designs for such firms as Liberty and Company, Piel Frères, Theodor Fahrner, and Unger Brothers. Often decorated with stylized plants, animals, humans, and exotic creatures, as well as historical scenes, belt buckles were popular accessories for women's fashion (fig. 16).

A similar example of the central element for this belt by Piel Frères was displayed at the Exposition Universelle in Paris in 1900. According to its provenance, the museum's belt was most likely originally owned by the Czech artist and designer Alphonse Mucha, who was active in Paris. ■

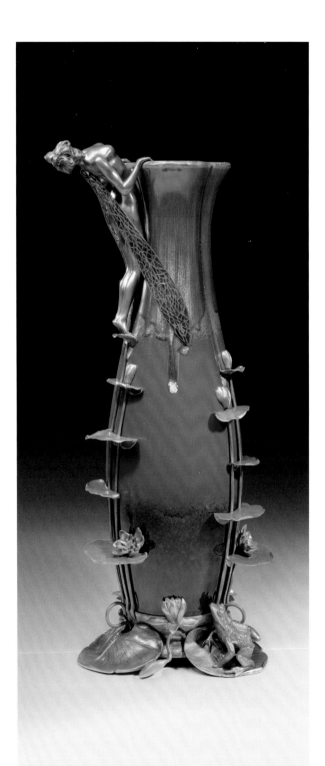

CHARLES PILLIVUYT PORCELAIN MANUFACTORY
French (Foëcy and Paris), 1853–1911
Mounts modeled by LOUIS CHALON
French, 1866–?
Wings enameled by EUGÈNE FEUILLÂTRE (?)
French, 1870–1916

Vase, 1898
Hard-paste porcelain, enamel, bronze, gilding
22 ½ x 10 ½ x 8 ½ in. (57.1 x 26.6 x 21 cm)
Inscribed (bottom): *Lamarre 1898 / Lt Fres;*
(bronze base rim): *LOUCHET*
Gift of Sydney and Frances Lewis, 85.49

This vase is an exceptional example of the collaboration among several artists in the late nineteenth century and is especially representative of Art Nouveau in both subject and style. The ceramic was made by Alphonse Adolphe Lamarre for the Charles Pillivuyt Porcelain Manufactory. The gilded-bronze mounts, which include lily pads, a frog, and a female figure, were modeled by sculptor Louis Chalon and cast by Charles Louchet. The figure's wings were most likely enameled by the notable Eugène Feuillâtre. The vase was displayed at the Salon of the Société Nationale des Beaux-Arts in Paris in 1898 and awarded a first prize. A similar example was exhibited at the Prima Esposizione Internazionale d'Arte Decorativa Moderna in Turin, Italy, in 1902. A third vase is in a private collection. ■

PAUL RANSON
French, 1864–1909
Silk embroidered by LAURE LACOMBE
French, 1834–1923

Fire Screen, ca. 1892
Mahogany, silk, stenciled dyes
60 ¾ x 8 ½ x 2 ⅜ in. (154.3 x 207 x 6 cm)
Gift of Sydney and Frances Lewis, 85.92

To create the central images for this screen, Paul Ranson first made a preparatory painting (which is now in a private collection) as well as a drawing (at the Petit Palais in Geneva). Artist Laure Lacombe, his close friend and mother of the French painter Georges Lacombe, then executed these designs in silk embroidery on the screen. The two female figures, a cat, and what may be a swan are intertwined with various arabesque motifs. The marquetry pattern of the wood is reminiscent of British designs of the period. This screen was displayed at the Salon of the Société Nationale des Beaux-Arts in Paris in 1899. ▪

PIERRE ROCHE
French, 1855–1922
Cast by E. GRUET JEUNE
French (Paris), active 1891–1904

Loïe Fuller, modeled 1894, made ca. 1901
Bronze
20 1/2 x 10 1/4 x 11 1/2 in. (52.1 x 26.7 x 29.2 cm)
Inscribed (bottom, front left): *PIERRE ROCHE*; (right): *LOÏE FULLER*
Marked: (base, right): *E. GRUET / JEUNE / FONDEUR /
. . . AVENUE DE CHATILLON PARIS*
Adolph D. and Wilkins C. Williams Fund, 86.124

During the 1890s, Loïe Fuller created a sensation when she performed her *Fire Dance*—the subject of this bronze sculpture—for audiences at the Folies-Bergère in Paris. According to artist Pierre Roche, "Miss Fuller has discovered an absolutely new art, which I can only call American. The light effects are those of the unique atmosphere of the Colorado canyons and only the Florida butterflies can compete with her in her grace movements and a chaste and diaphanous floating of her draperies."

Roche received many commissions for small- and large-scale sculptures, including the facade of Loïe Fuller's own theater at the 1900 Exposition Universelle in Paris. The only other bronze figure like VMFA's example is in the collection of the Musée des Arts Décoratifs in Paris; it was a gift from the children of Pierre Roche. The artist also exhibited a terracotta figure of Fuller at the Salon of the Société Nationale des Beaux-Arts in 1894, and several years later, another sculpture by Roche of the dancer was on view at the Salon in 1901. In addition to sculpture, Roche created ceramics, book bindings, metalwork, architectural decoration, and paintings. Loïe Fuller is represented in several other objects at VMFA, including a gilded-bronze lamp by Raoul François Larche. ■

This jar is an example of the well-known porcelain made by the Rozenburg Pottery Company beginning in 1899. Petal thin, it resembles English bone china in its composition and method of production. Pieces of Rozenburg porcelain that are related to this jar were displayed at the 1900 Exposition Universelle in Paris, where they were highly successful and received public acclaim. Samuel Schellink, a talented artist employed by Rozenburg, decorated this jar with flowers, trailing vines, and an elaborate peacock.

SAMUEL SCHELLINK
Dutch, 1876–1958
Made by ROZENBURG POTTERY COMPANY
Dutch (The Hague), 1883–1917

Covered Jar, 1913
Porcelain, enamel
14 ¼ x 4 ⅝ x 4 ⅝ in. (36.2 x 11.8 x 11.8 cm)
Inscribed (bottom): crown / *Rozenburg* / flower bird; *#638 / den Haag, sS*
Gift of Sydney and Frances Lewis, 85.43a–b

HENRI DE TOULOUSE-LAUTREC
French, 1864–1901
Printed by EDWARD ANCOURT
AND CIE
French (Paris)

La Revue Blanche, 1895
Lithograph
50 ¼ x 36 in. (127.6 x 91.4 cm)
Inscribed: artist's monogram / 95; Imp.
Edw. Ancourt, Paris
Sydney and Frances Lewis Art Nouveau
Fund, 72.7

La Revue Blanche was an influential artistic and literary magazine published in Paris between 1891 and 1903. This poster, created by the celebrated French artist Henri de Toulouse-Lautrec, depicts the Russian-born beauty Misia Natanson, wife of *La Revue Blanche* publisher Thadée Natanson. She was a model and muse to a number of French artists, including Pierre-Auguste Renoir, Édouard Vuillard, and Pierre Bonnard. VMFA has several other French Art Nouveau posters by artists such as Alphonse Mucha, Georges de Feure, Manuel Orazi, and Bonnard. ▪

This cachepot, or flowerpot holder, decorated with orchids represents a successful collaboration between an artist and a manufacturer of the late nineteenth century. Philippe Wolfers originally modeled several bronze vases in orchid shapes to decorate the interior of the Wolfers Frères Gallery in Antwerp (fig. 17). A number of vases were also displayed in Wolfers's stand at the International Exhibition in Brussels in 1897. After seeing the bronze cachepots there, employees from the firm of Émile Müller, a French specialist in ceramics, contacted Wolfers for permission to reproduce two cachepots and a vase in stoneware. The rich enamel glazes on the orchids and leaves of this vase enhance the sculptural forms as well as the shape of the bowl. Another example in stoneware was displayed at the Salon of the Société Nationale des Beaux-Arts in Paris in 1898. ▪

PHILIPPE WOLFERS
Belgian, 1858–1929
Made by ÉMILE MÜLLER ET CIE
French (Ivry, near Paris), founded 1854

Cachepot, designed 1896–97,
made 1897
Stoneware, enamel
14 1/2 x 19 x 18 1/2 in. (36.8 x 48.2 x 47 cm)
Inscribed (bottom): *Wolfers*
Sydney and Frances Lewis Art Nouveau
Fund, 81.27

Fig. 17: Wolfers Frères showroom, Antwerp, Belgium, ca. 1900. A bronze cachepot like the ceramic example at VMFA sits atop each cushioned sectional. Design Museum, Ghent

Sculptor and jeweler Philippe Wolfers was an apprentice in his father's silver studio. His sculpture, whether symbolic or realistic, was primarily inspired by nature. Here, the theme of good versus evil is expressed by the life-size swan struggling against an attacking snake in the center of the composition. With its wings upraised, the swan holds a cast-bronze elephant tusk. Wolfers considered this sculpture among his most important; he exhibited it in a number of major shows, including the 1899 Munich Secession and the 1902 Prima Esposizione Internazionale d'Arte Decorativa Moderna in Turin. The wood base was designed by the well-known Belgian architect Paul Hankar. ▪

PHILIPPE WOLFERS
Belgian, 1858–1929
Base designed by PAUL HANKAR
Belgian, 1859–1901

**The Song of the Swan
(Le Chant du Cygne),** 1898
Bronze, marble, oak, mahogany
Sculpture: 62 x 26 x 53 in. (157.4 x 66 x 134.5 cm)
Base: 35 x 38 x 53 in. (88.90 x 96.52 x 134.62 cm)
Adolph D. and Wilkins C. Williams Fund, 87.89

In favor of more modern approaches to art, Gustav Klimt, Josef Hoffmann, Koloman Moser, and others left the traditional Künstlerhaus (Society of Artists) in 1897 to form the Vienna Secession. A year later, architect and designer Joseph Maria Olbrich created an exhibition building for the group. The movement, known as Secessionism, was the Austrian version of Art Nouveau. Initially, objects of this style were curvilinear in form and decoration, but after 1900, Austrian artists were influenced by the straight lines and geometry of designs by Scottish architect Charles Rennie Mackintosh.

Hoffmann and Moser also cofounded the Wiener Werkstätte (Vienna Workshop), a designers' cooperative that was active from 1903 to 1932. Using the principles of the British Arts and Crafts movement, the Wiener Werkstätte provided well-designed, often handmade objects for a sophisticated and wealthy clientele. The workshop included departments for metalwork, bookbinding, leatherwork, cabinet-making, glass, ceramics, printing, fashion, and textiles, as well as an architectural office.

In late nineteenth-century Germany, the Art Nouveau style was known as Jugendstil (Youth Style), a term taken from the Munich-based art magazine *Jugend*. Influenced by the British Arts and Crafts movement, German designers adapted French floral motifs and Austrian geometric linear patterns to create their own distinct style. While the British Arts and Crafts practitioners rejected the use of machinery in the production of everyday objects, German designers embraced the machine in their desire to create quality design in furnishings and other works of art. This interest led to the development of modern industrial design and establishments such as the Bauhaus school.

AUSTRIAN and GERMAN ART NOUVEAU

LEOPOLD BAUER
Austrian, 1872–1938
Made by PORTOIS AND FIX
Austrian (Vienna), founded 1842

Cabinet, 1900
Sycamore, maple, various woods, brass, felt
35 ½ x 18 x 26 ½ in. (90.1 x 45.6 x
67.2 cm)
Marked (bottom): *Schl. No: 7013;* (bottom,
on paper label): *L. Nr 2142 R. Nr 3.0 /
10 – 1900;* (lock plate): *Portois & Fix /
Wien 7013*
Gift of Sydney and Frances Lewis, 85.79

This cabinet was designed by Leopold Bauer, a student of Austria's renowned revolutionary architect Otto Wagner. Featuring a marquetry pattern similar to British examples, it was most likely a private commission intended to hold a postcard collection. In 1901 the cabinet was displayed at an exhibition of decorative arts coordinated by the Vienna Secession, an organization of artists including Wagner who broke with traditional styles of the day. Bauer designed buildings, interior decoration, and furnishings in the Austrian Secessionist style. ▪

During his successful career, Peter Behrens designed buildings, interiors, furniture, metalwork, ceramics, textiles, and other objects. He played a major role in the founding of the Munich Seccession and the Vereinigte Werkstätten für Kunst im Handwerk (Unified Workshop for Art in Handicraft). In 1899, at the request of Ernst Ludwig, grand duke of Hesse, he helped create an artists' colony in Darmstadt, Germany. Later, Behrens was named artistic consultant for the largest electrical company in Berlin, AEG, where he was employed from 1907 to 1922, and he became one of Germany's leading industrial designers of objects for everyday use. This dining room chair is identical to six other examples that were part of a 1902 exhibition on modern living spaces at the Wertheim department store in Berlin (fig. 18).

PETER BEHRENS
German, 1868–1940

Chair, designed 1902, made 1903
Oak, replacement fabric
38 ¾ x 17 ¾ x 18 ¼ in. (98.4 x 45 x 46.3 cm)
Gift of Sydney and Frances Lewis, 85.138

Fig. 18: Interior decoration and furnishings designed by Peter Behrens for a dining room displayed at the Wertheim department store, Berlin, Germany, 1902. *Deutsche Kunst und Dekoration* (Germany, 1902–3)

JOSEF HOFFMANN
Austrian, 1870–1956
Made by JACOB AND JOSEF KOHN
Austrian, 1867–1914
For WIENER WERKSTÄTTE
Austrian (Vienna), 1903–1932

Chair, ca. 1904
Beech, leather
38 ¾ x 17 ½ x 17 in. (89.4 x 44.4 x 43.1 cm)
Sydney and Frances Lewis Art Nouveau Fund,
72.18

Fig. 19: Interior decoration and furnishings
designed by Josef Hoffmann for the dining
room of the Pürkersdorf Sanatorium, near
Vienna, Austria, ca. 1904. *The Studio Special
Edition* (London, 1906)

Mass-produced bentwood furniture was among the most important
developments in furniture design in the late nineteenth century. Following
Michael Thonet's 1830 steam-process experimentation, Jacob and Josef
Kohn made this chair according to Josef Hoffmann's design. Hoffmann
was commissioned by the Wiener Werkstätte between 1903 and 1906 to
design the Pürkersdorf Sanatorium, a fashionable spa near Vienna, and its
interiors and furnishings. This chair is one of about eighty that were made
for the dining room (fig. 19). Its geometric design elements are typical of
Hoffman's mature work.

JOSEF HOFFMANN
Austrian, 1870–1956
Made by KARL KALLERT
Austrian, 1879–(?)
For WIENER WERKSTÄTTE
Austrian (Vienna), 1903–1932

Clock, ca. 1903–4
Copper, alabaster, silver, coral
13 1/2 x 10 x 7 1/4 in. (34.3 x 25.3 x 19.4 cm)
Marked (back): *JH*, symbol for Wiener
Werkstätte, maker's mark for Karl Kallert,
rose mark
Adolph D. and Wilkins C. Williams Fund,
99.47

This rare clock was designed by the celebrated Austrian architect Josef Hoffmann. The body of the clock, with its series of cutout squares, is related to designs by Scottish architect Charles Rennie Mackintosh. In addition, the configuration of the numbers on the clock face is similar to Scottish examples. This piece was displayed in the Wiener Werkstätte showroom in Vienna soon after it was made.

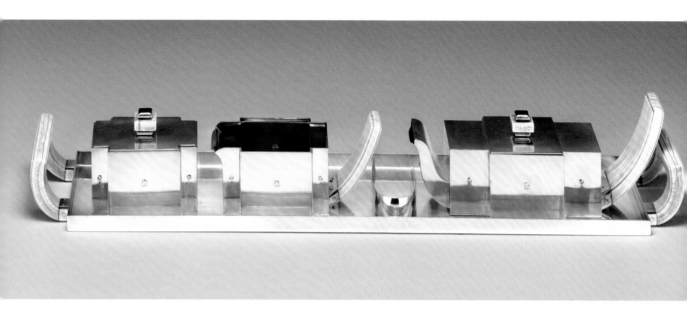

JOSEF HOFFMANN
Austrian, 1870–1956
Made by WIENER WERKSTÄTTE
Austrian (Vienna), 1903–1932

Tea Service, 1923
Silver, ivory
Tray: 2 3/8 x 23 5/8 x 4 13/16 in. (5.7 x 60 x 12.2 cm)
Teapot: 4 x 9 3/8 x 2 15/16 in. (10.2 x 23.8 x 7.5 cm)
Creamer: 3 1/8 x 6 1/4 x 2 5/8 in. (8 x 15.9 x 6.7 cm)
Tongs: 3 5/8 x 1 9/16 x 15/16 in. (9.2 x 4 x 2.5 cm)
Sugar bowl: 3 1/2 x 3 13/16 x 2 5/8 in. (9 x 9.87 x 6.7 cm)
Marked (each piece): *JH, WW, 900, MADE IN AUSTRIA, WIENER WERKSTATTE*
Gift of the Fabergé Society of the Virginia Museum of Fine Arts, 99.23.1–5a–b

This five-piece tea service, one of only three known to have been made, shows Josef Hoffmann's later style. An example of the service that was illustrated in a Wiener Werkstätte brochure of the period was priced at $650, a substantial amount at the time. An identical tea set, at the Los Angeles County Museum of Art, was sold by the American branch of the Wiener Werkstätte in New York City to the well-known early Hollywood screenwriter Frances Marion. ■

Patriz Huber received his basic training at the Kunstgewerbe School in Mainz, where his father was a teacher. In 1897 he went to Munich and studied interior decoration and arts and crafts. Some of his designs were reproduced in art magazines of the Darmstadt publisher Alexander Koch. Huber was subsequently appointed by Grand Duke Ernst Ludwig of Hess-Darmstadt to the artists' colony at the Mathildenhöhe. This rare buckle, one of the finest in VMFA's collection, is set with deep-green agate in a highly stylized and geometric plant-form design. ▪

PATRIZ HUBER
German, 1878–1902
Made by the firm of THEODOR FAHRNER
German (Pforzheim), active 1883–1919

Buckle, 1901
Silver, agate
1 ⅞ x 3 ½ in. (4.76 x 8.89 cm)
Marked (on reverse): *PH TF DEPOSÉ 935*
Swenson Art Nouveau Fund, 2005.6a–b

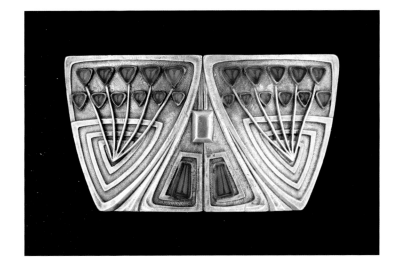

124

KOLOMAN MOSER
Austrian, 1868–1918
Made by JOHANN W. MÜLLER
Austrian, dates unknown

Armchair, 1902–3
Rosewood, maple, various woods, mother-of-pearl, replacement fabric
37 3/8 x 22 x 20 5/8 in. (94.9 x 55.8 x 52.3 cm)
Gift of Sydney and Frances Lewis, 85.80

This armchair was part of an impressive dining-room suite made for the apartment of Dr. Hans and Gerta Eisler von Terramare in Vienna, Austria. Koloman Moser, a highly influential Austrian artist of the period, designed the suite (now at the Badisches Landesmuseum in Karlsruhe, Germany). A prominent element, which became a hallmark of early twentieth-century Viennese furniture, is the use of repeated squares, as seen in the shape of the chair and the surface decoration. Another notable feature, one that sets this chair and the entire suite of furniture apart from more modest examples, is the rare and expensive material. A design in marquetry on the chair's back depicts a dove of peace. ▪

JOSEPH MARIA OLBRICH
Austrian, 1867–1908
Made by EDUARD HUECK
German (Lüdenscheid), founded 1814

Coffee and Tea Service, ca. 1904
Pewter, teak
Coffeepot: 7 ¾ x 4 ½ x 6 ¾ in. (19.1 x
11.4 x 17.1 cm)
Sugar bowl: 5 ⅛ x 4 ⅜ x 4 ⅜ in. (13 x
11.1 x 11.1 cm)
Teapot: 9 ¼ x 4 x 8 in. (23.5 x 10.1 x
20.8 cm)
Tray: 1 ⅝ x 22 ¾ x 14 ⅞ in. (4.1 x 57.8 x
37.7 cm)
Marked (each piece except tray, bottom):
EDELZINN / 1930 / E. Hueck; (coffeepot
and teapot, side): JO
Gift of Sydney and Frances Lewis, 85.280.1–4

In 1897 Joseph Maria Olbrich, a student of the distinguished Austrian architect Otto Wagner, joined Josef Hoffmann, Koloman Moser, and Gustav Klimt to found the Vienna Secession. One of Olbrich's first major commissions was the group's 1898 exhibition building. He moved to Darmstadt, Germany, in 1899 at the request of Ernst Ludwig, grand duke of Hesse, to help create the artists' colony in that city. Like many architects of his generation, Olbrich designed buildings, interiors, and objects, including clocks, furniture, textiles, and metalwork. An identical example of this coffee and tea service was displayed at a 1904 exhibition of the Künstlerkolonie (Artists' Colony) in Darmstadt and at the Louisiana Purchase Exposition held the same year in Saint Louis, Missouri. ▪

DAGOBERT PECHE
Austrian, 1887–1923

Wiener Werkstätte Poster for the Vienna Fair, 1921
Lithograph
37 1/2 x 23 3/4 in. (95.2 x 62.9 cm)
Inscribed: *D. PECHE*
Gift of Mrs. Jean Brown, 73.71.2

Dagobert Peche was a talented designer of the Wiener Werkstätte. From the time he joined this artists' collaborative in 1915 until his early death in 1923, Peche designed many objects, including lithographs like this one. He is considered to be among the most significant Austrian artists of the twentieth century.

Richard Riemerschmid, who designed architecture, interiors, furniture, ceramics, glass, metalwork, and textiles, took part in the founding of the Vereinigte Werkstätten für Kunst im Handwerk in Munich as well as the design collaborative Deutscher Werkbund. He was one of the most prolific designers in Germany in the late nineteenth and early twentieth centuries. This chair is identical to examples that were displayed in the German section at the Exposition Universelle in Paris in 1900. The construction relates to furniture made in England at this period, while the chair's curvilinear forms are characteristic of Jugendstil, the German version of Art Nouveau. VMFA also has blue-and-white stoneware designed by Riemerschmid. ▪

RICHARD RIEMERSCHMID
German, 1868–1957
Made by VEREINIGTE WERKSTÄTTEN
FÜR KUNST IM HANDWERK
German (Munich), founded 1898

Chair, 1898–99
Oak, leather
31 ¾ x 21 ¾ x 22 ½ in. (80.6 x 55.2 x 57.1 cm)
Gift of Sydney and Frances Lewis, 85.140

Otto Wagner, a prominent member of the Vienna Secession, is considered to be the founder of modern architecture and design in Vienna. His seminal 1895 textbook, *Modern Architecture*, influenced younger architects in Vienna and throughout Europe. In a 1903 competition, Wagner was awarded first prize for his design of the new Austrian Postal Savings Bank in Vienna. The building is regarded as a masterpiece of modern architecture. This chair was made for the bank's boardroom and is an early example of aluminum in Austrian furniture design.

OTTO WAGNER
Austrian, 1841–1918
Made by GEBRÜDER THONET
Austrian, 1853–1921

Armchair, ca. 1904
Beech, plywood, aluminum
30 ½ x 21 ⅞ x 22 in. (77.5 x 55.6 x 55.9 cm)
Sydney and Frances Lewis Art Nouveau Fund, 84.82

Fig. 20: Boardroom, Österreichische Postsparkasse (Austrian Postal Savings Bank), Vienna, designed by Otto Wagner. *Fünfundzwanzig Jahre Postsparkasse* (Vienna, 1908)

HENRY VAN DE VELDE
Belgian, 1863–1957
Made by KOCH AND BERGFELD
German (Bremen), founded 1829
For THEODOR MÜLLER
German (Weimar), 1863–after 1945

Jardiniere and Two Candelabra,
1902–3
Silver
Jardiniere: 5 ¾ x 17 ½ x 9 ½ in. (14.5 x
44.4 x 24.1 cm)
Candelabra (4): 15 ½ x 9 x 5 ½ in. (39.3 x
22.8 x 13.9 cm) (each)
Marked (each piece, bottom): *TH MÜLLER
925*
Sydney and Frances Lewis Art Nouveau
Fund, 72.14.1–3/5

In 1902 Theodor Müller, a major silversmith and jewelry company in
Weimar, Germany, was commissioned by the Thuringian State (Saxe-
Weimar) to make a 353-piece silver service for Wilhelm Ernst, grand duke
of Saxe-Weimar-Eisenach, on the occasion of his wedding to Caroline
Reuss of Greiz. The service was designed by Henry van de Velde and
included a 250-piece set of flatware and serving utensils as well as three
jardinieres, eight candelabra, six sauce boats, twelve salt cellars, eighteen
serving trays, and fifty-six plates.

The craftsmen at Theodor Müller made plaster models of the jardinieres
following van de Velde's specifications. The models were sent to Koch and
Bergfeld in Bremen, where they were used to form objects in silver. The
museum's jardiniere and four candelabra (two pictured) may be from the
grand ducal service or from another commission, such as the silver wedding
service ordered in 1903 by Wilhelma, marquise de Biron, sister of the
important German art patron Count Harry Kessler. ◼

HENRY VAN DE VELDE
Belgian, 1863–1957
Made by THEODOR MÜLLER
German (Weimar), 1863–after 1945

Buckle, 1902
Silver
2 x 4 ⅛ in. (6 x 10.5 cm)
Marked (both halves): artist's hallmark, half
moon, crown, *800, TM, DEPOSÉ*
Sydney and Frances Lewis Endowment Fund
and Gift of Dr. Karl and Gisela Kreuzer,
2004.4a–b

In 1902, architect and designer Henry van de Velde collaborated with the Theodor Müller company. The same year, van de Velde also established a craft seminar in Weimer that later became the Grand Ducal School of Arts and Crafts in 1907. Belt buckles designed by van de Velde are rare; only five examples are known today (although two have disappeared). VMFA also has a jardiniere and four candelabra designed by van de Velde and made by Theodor Müller. ■

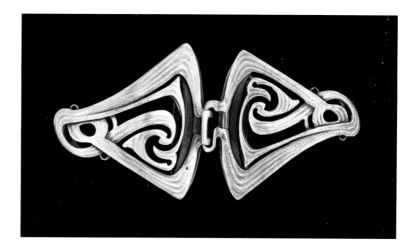

The Art Deco style, an international phenomenon, flourished from just before World War I to about 1935. The term, coined in the 1960s, derives from the title of a 1925 exhibition held in Paris— Exposition Internationale des Arts Décoratifs et Industriels Modernes (International Exhibition of Modern and Industrial Decorative Arts). The exhibition established France as the world's leader in design and fashion. At this period, artists and craftsmen working in the Art Deco style believed that handcraftsmanship was superior to machine manufacture. They used only the finest materials and decorative treatments to create luxurious furnishings and valued modern and up-to-date designs. Many so-called traditionalists were inspired by historical styles, such as mid-eighteenth-century rococo or late eighteenth-century neoclassicism. Other artists were more forward looking, an interest that eventually lead to industrial design or mass production.

There were a number of major historical and cultural influences that affected the design aesthetic of this period. In 1909, for example, Serge Diaghilev introduced the Ballets Russes in Paris, and the color and flair of the stage sets greatly influenced many leading Art Deco designers. Similarly, archaeological discoveries in Egypt prompted new interest in the historical styles from other regions and in materials such as ivory, lacquer, sharkskin, and snakeskin.

The Art Deco collection at VMFA is one of the finest and most extensive in an American museum. Many talented French Art Deco designers, such as Émile-Jacques Ruhlmann, Pierre Legrain, Eileen Gray, Jean Dunand, and Süe et Mare are represented in the museum's collection by iconic examples of their work.

ART DECO

Fig. 21: Salon at Jacques Doucet's Studio Saint-James, Neuilly, France.
L'Illustration (Paris, May 1930)

JACQUES DOUCET: ART PATRON

The Art Deco style was especially popular among the fashionable well-to-do in France. One such proponent was the renowned fashion designer Jacques Doucet, who was also an important art patron. Following aristocratic French taste, Doucet first collected eighteenth-century art and furnishings for his sumptuous townhouse on the rue Spotini in Paris. However, he later rejected this traditional eighteenth-century style and patronized the most progressive artists and designers of the early twentieth century. With his highly refined taste, he eventually formed one of the most significant collections of avant-garde art at the time. In 1912, he sold his major collection of eighteenth-century art and acquired contemporary paintings by Pablo Picasso, Henri Matisse, Amedeo Modigliani, Henri Rousseau, and others.

At the same time, Doucet commissioned the designer Paul Poiret, his company Atelier Martine, and Paul Iribe to decorate his new Paris apartment, on the avenue du Bois de Boulogne (now avenue Foch), in the Art Deco style. Iribe hired the most innovative designers of the day. In 1914, he left France for the United States, and Doucet later engaged Pierre Legrain, a designer and bookbinder, in the mid-1920s to complete the interior decoration of his new Studio Saint-James, attached to his residence in the Paris suburb of Neuilly-sur-Seine. This suite of rooms is celebrated today as a masterpiece of Art Deco (fig. 21). Ten objects from Doucet's Art Deco collection are part of the VMFA collection.

ROSE ADLER
French, 1890–1959

Table, ca. 1926
Ebony, sharkskin, metal, enamel
29 ¾ x 27 ¾ x 15 ⅝ in. (75.5 x 70.5 x 39.7 cm)
Gift of Sydney and Frances Lewis, 85.93

Fig. 22: Salon at Jaques Doucet's Studio Saint-James, Neuilly, France. *L'Illustration* (Paris, May 1930)

In 1917 Rose Adler began studying at the École du Comité des Dames of the Union Centrale Arts Décoratifs in Paris. She later became a highly respected designer of bookbindings. The couturier Jacques Doucet bought several examples of her bindings and also commissioned furniture and ornamental boxes from her. She made this ebony table for Doucet using exotic sharkskin to depict a fantasy cityscape of stairs, arches, and streetlights. It appears in a photograph of the salon at Doucet's Studio Saint-James in Neuilly, a suburb of Paris (fig. 22). ▪

During the 1920s, the art of bookbinding reached new heights of excellence in design. Both the front and back covers of a book were equal in importance to the actual contents. Three artists collaborated to create this book, *Cheri*: Colette wrote the text, Marcel Vertès produced the engravings, and Rose Adler designed the binding. Adler also designed bookbindings for Jacques Doucet, and, after his death in 1929, she continued to work for the Jacques Doucet Literary Foundation. ■

ROSE ADLER
French, 1890–1959

Bookbinding, 1931
Edition 48/100, Editions de la Roseraie, Paris
Morocco leather, engraving
11 x 9 x 1 ⅞ in. (28 x 23 x 4.8 cm)
Inscribed (inside front cover): *Rose Adler 1931;* (inside back cover): *To Jeanne Dor*
Gift of Sydney and Frances Lewis, 85.37a–b

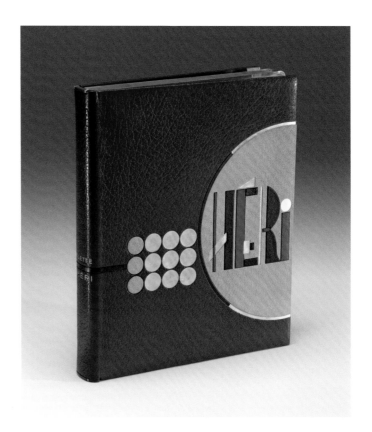

EMILE JUST BACHELET
French, 1892–1981

Venus and Love, ca. 1934
Ivory, bronze, gilding, marble
49 x 13 in. (124.4 x 33 cm)
Inscribed (base, back): *E. J. BACHELET*
Gift of Sydney and Frances Lewis, 85.314

Ivory was a significant import for European countries, especially Belgium and France, both of which had colonies in Africa. Emile Just Bachelet, well known for his life-size animal sculptures carved in stone and bronze, also made objects in ivory. In this example, Bachelet skillfully carved from a tusk a nude Venus holding a small figure of Love. The sculpture was displayed in Paris at the 1934 Salon of the Société des Artistes Décorateurs (Society of Artists-Decorators) and later in their pavilion at the 1937 Exposition Internationale des Arts et Techniques dans la Vie Moderne (International Exhibition of Arts and Techniques in Modern Art).

GEORGE BARBIER
French, 1882–1932
Engraved by HENRI REIDEL

The Taste for Lacquer (Le goût des laques), ca. 1920–24
Engraved print with pochoir (stencil) colors
from a portfolio of decorated paper wrappers, 2 illustrated pages, table of contents page, and 16 stencil prints
Inscribed (each plate): *George Barbier*
13 x 18 in. (32 x 45 cm)
Purchased with funds provided by John and Maria Shugars in memory of Christine Louise (Dittmer) Shugars, 2009.341.10/16

George Barbier was the most influential French Art Deco fashion illustrator. Beginning in 1912, he regularly contributed designs to fashion magazines such as *Journal des Dames et des Modes* and *Gazette du Bon Ton*. He also worked for the theater and cinema, designing the costumes worn by Rudolph Valentino in the 1924 Hollywood film *Monsieur Beaucaire*. This plate is from Barbier's well-known *Le Bonheur du Jour, ou Les Grâces à la mode*, a portfolio of stenciled color prints. Created from 1920 to 1924, the individual prints depict ladies and gentlemen dressed in the latest Paris fashions while engaged in amusements of the day. This print shows a fashionable interior with an elaborate lacquer screen behind two very stylish women. VMFA has numerous other stenciled prints by Barbier that are part of the rare book collection. ▪

During the 1920s, Edgar Brandt and other artists created metalwork in a highly decorative manner. Brandt was a major artist who was represented at the Exposition Internationale des Arts Décoratifs et Industriels Modernes held in Paris in 1925, by which time he had earned great acclaim. He designed lamps, gates, architectural features, radiator grilles, andirons, and other objects for a number of buildings at the Paris exhibition as well as for his own showroom. This pair of gates decorated an interior entrance hall of a building on the rue Guynemer in Paris. They were initially exhibited at the Salon of the Société des Artistes Décorateurs in Paris in 1926. Although wrought iron is a heavy material, Brandt's design here resulted in intertwined tendrils that seem light and airy. ■

EDGAR BRANDT
French, 1880–1960

Pair of Gates, 1926
Wrought iron
42 x 72 in. (106.7 x 182.9 cm)
Marked (front, top): *E. BRANDT*
Gift of Sydney and Frances Lewis
85.277.1–2

René Buthaud was the most prominent French ceramist of the 1920s and 1930s. Appointed a jury member of the 1925 Paris Exposition, he was later a professor of decoration at the École des Beaux-Arts in Bordeaux in 1931. Like many Art Deco designers, Buthaud had eclectic taste and sought inspiration from contemporary art as well as African and Oceanic art, which he collected. His interest in non-Western culture, which was shared by Pablo Picasso, Georges Braque, and other artists of the early twentieth century, is evident in the sculpture painted on this vase— a carved-wood statue on which a young woman rests. It is possible that the statue was part of the artist's personal collection.

RENÉ BUTHAUD
French, 1886–1986

Oceania Vase, ca. 1931
Glazed and enameled stoneware
17 ½ x 9 ½ in. (44.5 x 24 cm)
Marked (bottom): *RB*
Sydney and Frances Lewis Endowment Fund, 2010.105

Buthaud's *Oceania Vase* was displayed, along with his *Africa Vase* (at the Metropolitan Museum of Art, New York), in the Metropolitan Pavilion at the Exposition Coloniale Internationale (International Colonial Exhibition) held in Paris in 1931, the last world's fair exclusively devoted to the celebration of international colonialism. After the exhibition closed in November 1931, both vases were on view later that year in the Exposition des Artisans Français Contemporains (Exhibition of Contemporary French Artisans) at the Galerie Rouard in Paris. ▪

ALBERT CHEURET
French, 1884–1966

Clock, ca. 1929
Silvered bronze, onyx
6 ¼ x 16 ½ x 4 in. (15.9 x 41.9 x 10.1 cm)
Inscribed (front, left): *Albert Cheuret*
Gift of Sydney and Frances Lewis, 85.218

When the tomb of Pharaoh Tutankhamen was discovered in 1922, an international craze for all things Egyptian ensued. The exotic nature and geometric lines of the ancient Egyptian style appealed to artists of the period. Cheuret's clock is a well-known Art Deco object in the Egyptian style. Its pyramidal shape is similar to an Egyptian headdress or wig with angular hair flanking the face. The clock's numbers were meant to suggest hieroglyphics. ▪

In 1912, after three years of studying sculpture in Italy, Demêtre Chiparus moved to Paris, where he lived the remainder of his life. Sculptures by Chiparus are classic examples of the Art Deco style. His specialty was combining cast bronze and ivory, a technique called chryselephantine. Dancers of the Ballets Russes as well as actors from French theater and early films were among his most notable subjects, typically rendered as long, slender, and stylized figures. Like other artists, Chiparus was influenced by Egyptian art after the discovery of Pharaoh Tutankhamen's tomb in 1922. His sculptures combine elegance and luxury, embodying the spirit of the period, and demonstrate the French tradition of high-quality decorative arts. VMFA currently has several other sculptures by Chiparus.

DEMÊTRE CHIPARUS
Romanian (active in France),
1886–1947

Eternal Friends, ca. 1928
Cold-painted bronze, ivory, onyx
16 ½ x 16 ¾ x 3 ⅞ in. (41.9 x 42.5 x
9.8 cm)
Inscribed (bottom, top left): *Chiparus*
Gift of Sydney and Frances Lewis, 85.332

MARCEL COARD
French, 1889–1975

Sofa, ca. 1925
Rosewood, ivory, leather
34 ½ x 96 x 36 in. (87.6 x 243.8 x
91.5 cm)
Inscribed (back, right edge): *M Coard*
Gift of Sydney and Frances Lewis, 85.99

Fig. 23: Salon at Jacques Doucet's Studio
Saint-James, Neuilly, France. *L'Illustration*
(Paris, May 1930)

Marcel Coard studied architecture at the École des Beaux-Arts in Paris
before opening a gallery on the city's boulevard Haussmann. A leading
Art Deco designer, he made furniture for such notable clients as fashion
designer Jacques Doucet. This sofa, owned by Doucet, was carved in
rosewood to resemble rattan, evidence of Coard's interest in African and
Far Eastern art. It was placed first in Doucet's apartment on the avenue du
Bois de Boulogne (now avenue Foch) in Paris and later moved to the salon
of his Studio Saint-James, located in the Paris suburb of Neuilly, where it
sat under Henri Rousseau's painting *The Snake Charmer*. Other furnishings
in the room included objects by Eileen Gray and Pierre Legrain; a pair of
glass doors by René Lalique; and paintings by Amedeo Modigliani, Pablo
Picasso, and Georges Braque (fig. 23). VMFA also has a bedroom suite
by Coard that was commissioned in 1929 by Paul Cocteau, brother of the
celebrated French writer Jean Cocteau, for his residence at Champgault,
near Tours, France. ■

DONALD DESKEY
American, 1894–1989
Made by DESKEY-VOLLMER, INC.
American (New York, New York),
1927–31

Three-Panel Screen, ca. 1928
Oil on canvas, metal leaf, wood
77 ¾ x 58 ¾ x 1 ¼ in. (197.5 x 149.2 x
2.9 cm)
Marked (back, on paper label): *Modern
Decorative Art / Deskey-Vollmer / New York*
Gift of the Sydney and Frances Lewis
Foundation, 85.62

In the 1920s Donald Deskey was part of a group of American designers influenced by European Art Deco. He designed several important interiors, including those in New York City's landmark Radio City Music Hall. Besides public buildings, Deskey's commissions included interior decoration for numerous private houses. One of them, owned by Glendon Allvine, was promoted in the press as "America's First Modernistic Home." VMFA's screen, initially owned by Allvine, follows the color scheme of the dining room. Deskey also designed well-known packaging for popular American household products such as Crest toothpaste. ■

FÉLIX DEL MARLE
French, 1889–1952

Suite of Furniture, 1926
Painted wood, frosted glass, metallic paint,
fabric, painted metal
Sofa, bar/coffee table, armchairs (3),
chandeliers (2, not shown), lamp
Sofa: 29 1/2 x 66 1/8 x 27 9/16 in. (75 x 168 x
70 cm)
Bar/coffee table: 22 1/16 x 22 3/4 x 16 1/8 in.
(56 x 67 x 41 cm)
Armchairs: 24 13/16 x 33 1/16 x 30 5/16 in. (63 x
84 x 77 cm) (each)
Chandeliers: 21 1/4 x 26 3/8 x 20 1/2 in. (55 x
67 x 52 cm) (each)
Lamp: 64 15/16 x 17 3/4 x 9 7/8 in. (165 x 45 x
25 cm)
Gift of Sydney and Frances Lewis,
85.101.1–8

In 1913 French artist Félix Del Marle published his "Manifeste futuriste à Montmartre" ("Futurist Manifesto against Montmartre") in the *Paris-Journal*. Although he was not Italian, he was accepted by the Italian Futurists, a group of painters, poets, sculptors, and architects who glorified technology, war, and other aspects of modern life. After World War I, Del Marle met followers of the Dutch De Stijl movement and adopted their philosophy, which emphasized the use of primary colors, straight lines, rectangles, and squares. Working with De Stijl theory, Del Marle made this suite of furniture for his own house at Pont-sur-Sambre in Bécon, France (fig. 24).

Fig. 24: Interior of Félix Del Marle residence, Pont-sur-Sambre, Bécon, France, ca. 1930. Virginia Museum of Fine Arts

Lacquered by JEAN DUNAND
Swiss (active in France), 1877–1942
Designed by PIERRE LEGRAIN
French, 1889–1929

Cabinet, ca. 1925
Lacquer, wood, pewter, bronze
33 ⅞ x 29 ⅛ x 13 ¼ in. (86 x 74 x 33.7 cm)
Gift of Sydney and Frances Lewis, 85.121

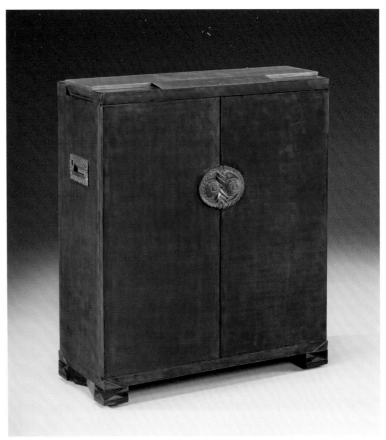

Pierre Legrain designed this cabinet for the fashion designer Jacques Doucet. Its interior has twenty-four small file drawers covered in light-red lacquer. Each drawer has a metal handle with a designated letter of the alphabet. Based on Asian models, the cabinet was most likely made for Doucet's financial records. It was probably first displayed at Doucet's apartment on the avenue du Bois de Boulogne (now avenue Foch) and later at his Studio Saint-James in Neuilly. Legrain's influence was critical in the interior decoration and furnishings of Doucet's houses, an ongoing project from 1914 to 1929. ■

Furniture designers of the 1920s were inspired by Japanese lacquerware. A lengthy and challenging technique, lacquering required skill and patience. Natural lacquer, from the sap of *Rhus succedanea* (Japanese wax tree) and *Rhus vernicifera* (Japanese lacquer tree), was mixed with different pigments and minerals to create various colors. Metal foils or powders, mother-of-pearl, or crushed eggshells were also added for decoration. The process required many coats of lacquer. After one coat dried, the surface was carefully polished with pumice before the next coat was applied.

JEAN DUNAND
Swiss (active in France), 1877–1942

Pair of Armchairs, 1925
Lacquer, wood, silver, replacement fabric
32 x 28 x 30 ¼ in. (81.3 x 71.1 x 76.8 cm) (each)
Gift of Sydney and Frances Lewis, 85.102.1–2

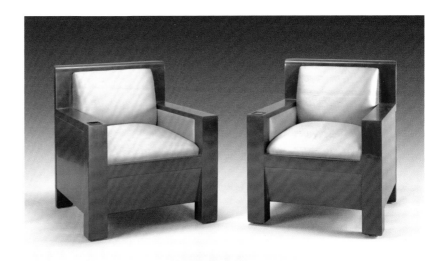

In 1912 Jean Dunand studied the technique with the Japanese master Seizo Sugawara. After 1918, with the help of Indo-Chinese craftsmen, Dunand established a large workshop for lacquer. He first exhibited lacquer objects in 1921 and regularly made furniture, screens, vases, and jewelry in this manner. Later, he collaborated on the interior decoration of two transatlantic steamships: the *Atlantique* (1931) and the ill-fated *Normandie* (1935).

These lacquered armchairs are identical to examples in black that were made for the French Embassy smoking room, part of the Pavilion of the Société des Artistes Décorateurs, at the Exposition Internationale des Arts Décoratifs et Industriels Modernes in Paris in 1925.

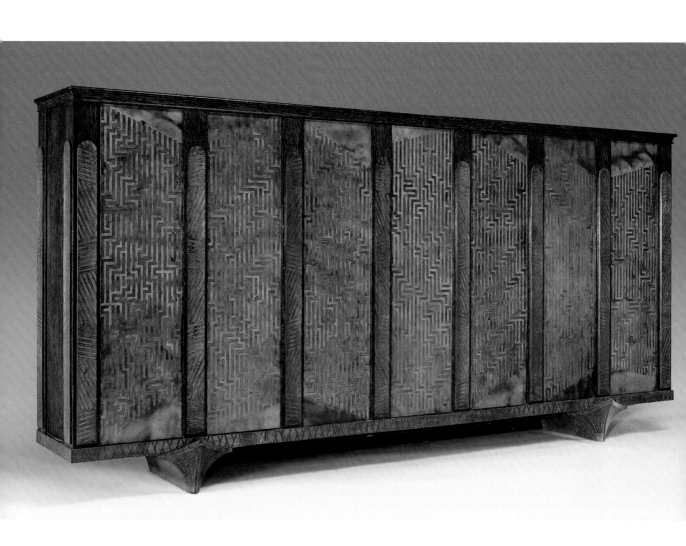

This impressive bookcase combines the talents of two distinguished Art Deco artists. Jean Dunand decorated the seven doors with inlaid copper and silver. Mounted on pivots, they open to reveal sycamore-lined adjustable shelves. The designer, Eugène Printz, regularly displayed his furniture at exhibitions in Paris and received many commissions from important patrons such as French fashion designer Jeanne Lanvin. A similar bookcase was on view at the Salon des Tuileries in Paris in 1944 and at the Salon of the Société des Artistes Décorateurs in Paris in 1947.

Decorated by JEAN DUNAND
Swiss (active in France), 1877–1942
Designed by EUGÈNE PRINTZ
French, 1889–1948

Bookcase, ca. 1937
Palm wood, copper, silver, sycamore
57 x 121 ⅝ x 19 ¾ in. (144.7 x 308.9 x 50.2 cm)
Gift of Sydney and Frances Lewis, 85.126

JEAN DUPAS
French, 1882–1964
Printed by ROUSSEAU FRÈRES
French (Bordeaux)

The Student's Ball (Bal des Étudiants), 1927
Lithograph
79 X 50½ in. (200.66 x 127.32 cm)
Inscribed: *Rousseau Frères Imp. Bordeaux, Jean Dupas 1926*
John and Maria Shugars Fund, 2010.110

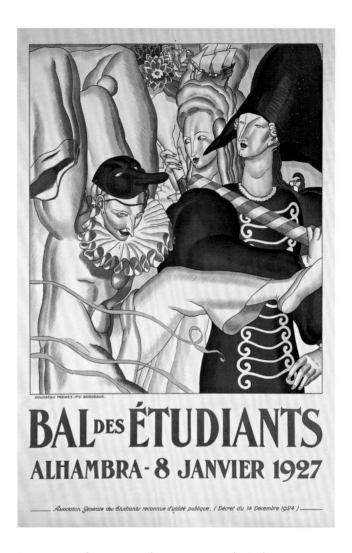

Jean Dupas, born in Bordeaux, was a talented Art Deco artist. He created his first poster for the Salon of the Société des Artistes Décorateurs in Paris in 1924 and thereafter received regular commissions. This poster was printed by Rousseau Frères, a renowned establishment in Bordeaux capable of creating vivid colors. The scene evokes the annual Venetian Carnival, with its mix of traditional commedia dell'arte costumes and late eighteenth-century fashion. Only a small number of these posters were produced, most likely because of the high cost of printing such fine colors. ▪

JEAN FOUQUET
French, 1899–1984
Made by MAISON GEORGES
FOUQUET
French (Paris), 1895–1936

Bracelet, designed 1926,
made ca. 1929
Gold, platinum, diamonds, enamel, jade
1 x 6 ⅞ x ⅜ in. (2.6 x 17.3 x 1 cm)
Inscribed: *JEAN FOUQUET, 21705*
Marked: dog's head, eagle's head (twice),
rhinoceros's head, *GF,* vertical lozenge,
whip and arrow symbol
Gift of Sydney and Frances Lewis, 85.237

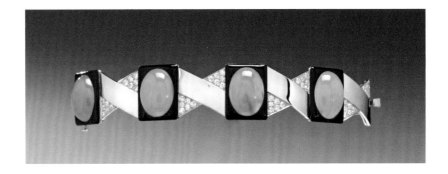

Jean Fouquet began working for his family's jewelry firm in Paris in 1919. A company with a long and distinguished history, it was established by Fouquet's grandfather Alphonse in 1860. During the 1920s and 1930s, Jean Fouquet created highly innovative Art Deco jewelry, examples of which he first displayed at the Exposition Internationale des Arts Décoratifs et Industriels Modernes in Paris in 1925.

This bracelet was originally shown at an exhibition titled *Les Arts de la bijouterie, joaillerie et orfèvrerie* at the Musée Galliera in Paris in 1929. It has abstract and geometric shapes and is set with precious and semiprecious stones. To mark the emperor of Ethiopia's visit to France in 1936, the French president presented a bracelet of this design to the emperor's wife.

JEAN GOULDEN
French, 1878–1946

Clock, 1929
Silvered bronze, enamel, marble
19 ½ x 8 x 7 ½ in. (49.5 x 20.3 x 19 cm)
Inscribed (back, bottom): *XLVII 29 JEAN
GOULDEN*
Gift of Sydney and Frances Lewis, 85.219

Jean Goulden's clock, with its geometric shapes and lines, is typical of French Art Deco. The artist was fascinated by the Byzantine enamels he discovered at Mount Athos in Greece. Goulden, who made about 150 objects in silver and enamel, was taught by the master enameler and lacquerer Jean Dunand, whose work is represented in the VMFA collection. The museum also has a silvered-bronze and enamel lamp by Goulden. ▪

EILEEN GRAY
Irish (active in France), 1878–1976

Lamp, 1923
Lacquer, wood, painted parchment shade
(modern replacement), electrical parts
73 x 20 ½ in. (185.4 x 52 cm)
Gift of Sydney and Frances Lewis,
85.169a–c

Born in Ireland, Eileen Gray studied drawing at the Slade School of Art in London, where she became intrigued by Japanese lacquer. After moving to Paris in 1902, she learned the technique from Japanese master Seizo Sugawara. Though never formally trained in furniture design, Gray created multi-paneled lacquered screens that attracted the attention of art patrons. One of her earliest clients was the fashion designer Jacques Doucet, who commissioned several pieces after seeing Gray's screen at the Salon of the Société des Artistes Décorateurs in Paris in 1913. Gray also made other types of furniture using lacquer and a variety of decorative techniques. By 1922 she had opened a Paris art gallery, Jean Désert, where she sold her own work.

In 1923 Gray designed a "Bedroom-boudoir for Monte Carlo" as part of the Salon of the Société des Artistes Décorateurs. This futuristic floor lamp was included in the display, along with carpets, tables, sofas, screens, and other lighting fixtures. It shows Gray's skill as a lacquerer as well as her ability to design furniture that was progressive in style. The lamp's form was influenced by art from both the South Sea Islands and Africa. It was acquired by Madame Juliette Mathieu Lévy from Gray's art gallery in Paris. ▪

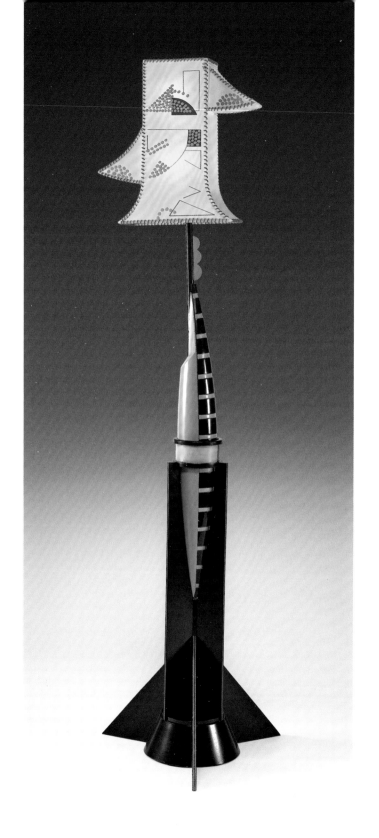

EILEEN GRAY
Irish (active in France), 1878–1976

Pirogue Chaise Longue, 1919–20
Lacquer, wood, silver leaf, replacement fabric
28 3/8 x 106 5/16 x 25 9/16 in. (72.1 x 270 x 64.9 cm)
Gift of Sydney and Frances Lewis, 85.112

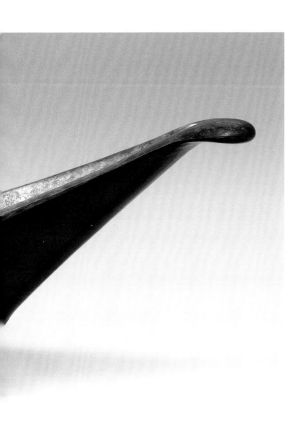

This rare and unusual chaise longue, inspired by Polynesian and Micronesian dugout canoes (*pirogues* in French), is lacquered and silvered. Very similar to one that Gray designed in 1919–20 for Madame Juliette Mathieu Lévy, who owned the successful Paris fashion establishment called Suzanne Talbot, it is among the most celebrated examples of French Art Deco furniture. The museum's chaise longue was purchased by Mr. and Mrs. Jacques-Henri Labourdette from Gray's art gallery in Paris in 1930.

ANDRÉ GROULT
French, 1884–1967

Chair, 1925
Sharkskin, wood, replacement fabric
31 ½ x 19 ½ x 20 ½ in. (80 x 49.5 x
52 cm)
Gift of Sydney and Frances Lewis, 85.116

One of the pavilions at the 1925 Exposition Internationale des Arts
Décoratifs et Industriels Modernes in Paris represented a French embassy.
The building's twenty-five interiors, arranged around a central court, were
furnished by well-known members of the Société des Artistes Décorateurs,
including André Groult. All of the furniture by Groult was curved in form
and decorated in sharkskin, a material that the artist often used in his
designs. Groult made this chair for a room identified as the "Bedroom of
the Wife of the French Ambassador." He also worked on other displays for
the exhibition, including those by the Fontaine et Cie, Christofle-Baccarat,
Les Arts du Jardin, and the Société de l'Art Appliqué aux Métiers. ▪

ANDRÉ GROULT
French, 1884–1967

Sideboard, ca. 1913
Ebony, sharkskin, ivory
39 3/8 x 25 1/2 x 60 1/2 in. (100 x 64.8 x
153.7 cm)
Gift of Sydney and Frances Lewis, 85.117

Born in Paris, André Groult exhibited his furniture at the salons from
about 1910 through the 1930s. As this sideboard reflects, he admired
the unusual qualities of sharkskin—such as the texture and gradation of
colors—and often used it in his furniture. The date of the sideboard is
based on the date of a desk at the Musée des Arts Décoratifs in Paris with
similar column-like legs ornamented with ivory details. That desk was
displayed at the Salon d'Autumne (Autumn Salon) in 1913. ▪

166

RENÉ LALIQUE
French, 1860–1945

Panel, designed 1928, made 1929
Molded glass, acid-etched glass, sycamore
Central panels (3): 17 ¾ x 5 ¹¹/₁₆ in. (45 x
14.5 cm) (each)
Top and bottom panels (6): 4 ⅜ x 5 ¹¹/₁₆ in.
(11 x 14.5 cm) (each)
Gift of Sydney and Frances Lewis, 85.350

René Lalique was a highly talented goldsmith and jeweler who enjoyed a second career as a successful glassmaker. He achieved his greatest recognition in the latter profession at the Exposition Internationale des Arts Décoratifs et Industriels Modernes in Paris in 1925, where his varied glass was displayed throughout the French pavilions. Lalique's glass objects also included elements for the interiors of trains, such as the sleeping car on the President of France (1923) and the Pullman car on the Côte d'Azur train (1929). This glass panel, which depicts men and women dancing among grapes and grapevines, served as a partition at one end of that Pullman car. ▪

LE CORBUSIER
(CHARLES ÉDOUARD JEANNERET)
Swiss (active in France), 1887–1965
PIERRE JEANNERET
Swiss (active in France), 1896–1967
CHARLOTTE PERRIAND
French, 1903–1999

Armchair, designed 1928, made
ca. 1929
Chromed tubular steel, metal, fabric
25 x 23 ¼ x 24 ¾ in. (63.5 x 59 x 63 cm)
Sydney and Frances Lewis Endowment
Fund, 88.127

Architect Le Corbusier defined the house as "a machine for living in" and
furniture as "machines for sitting." This armchair, an icon of twentieth-century
furniture design, is considered his masterpiece. In 1929, Le Corbusier and
architect Charlotte Perriand designed seating for a house in Ville d'Avary
in France, which included an armchair with a tilting back; VMFA's example
is based on that model. Another chair of the same design was initially
displayed at the Salon d'Autumne in Paris in 1929. Composed of eight
individual sections of tubular steel, the chair was costly to produce and of
limited production. ▪

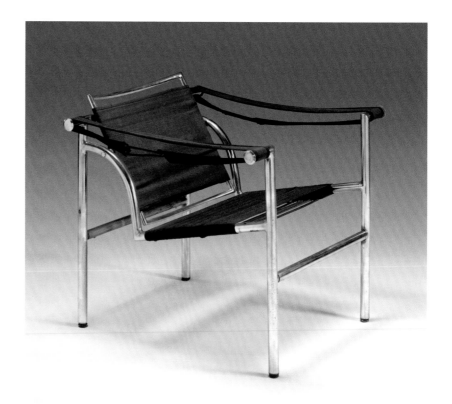

PIERRE LEGRAIN
French, 1889–1929

Birdcage on Stand, ca. 1922–23
Lacquer, wood, parchment, aluminum
57 ½ x 22 ½ x 22 ½ in. (146 x 57 x 57 cm)
Sydney and Frances Lewis Endowment
Fund, 89.23a–b

Fig. 25: **Design for a Birdcage,** ca. 1922–
23, Pierre Legrain, pencil, ink, and gouache
on paper, 17 ⅞ x 11 ⅞ in. (45.4 x 30.2 cm).
John and Maria Shugars Fund, 2013.7

This birdcage on stand decorated the entrance hall of the Studio Saint-James, an addition to Jacques Doucet's house in the Neuilly suburb of Paris. It was first on view at Doucet's Paris apartment on the avenue du Bois de Boulogne (now avenue Foch). Pierre Legrain used aluminum wires for the cage and lacquered wood for its frame, perches, and stand. He trimmed the cage with parchment—traditionally reserved for books—and also wrapped it around the feet, handles, and stretcher. Artists during this period favored aluminum and lacquer in their furnishings. VMFA also has a preliminary design by Legrain for this birdcage (fig. 25).

PIERRE LEGRAIN
French, 1889–1929

Stool, ca. 1923
Lacquer, sharkskin, wood
21 x 21 x 12 in. (53.4 x 53.4 x 30.5 cm)
Gift of Sydney and Frances Lewis, 85.123

Fig. 26: Salon at Jacques Doucet's Studio
Saint-James, Neuilly, France, ca. 1929–30,
silver gelatin photograph. Sydney and
Frances Lewis Endowment Fund, 2013.10

This unusual stool, displayed at the Salon of the Société des Artistes
Décorateurs in Paris in 1923, was inspired by an example from the Asante
people of Ghana. It was part of Jacques Doucet's furnishings at his Paris
apartment on the avenue du Bois de Boulogne (now avenue Foch) and
was later moved to his Studio Saint-James in Neuilly (fig. 26), a suburb
of Paris. ▪

This tabouret by Pierre Legrain, originally owned by Jacques Doucet, was inspired by stools made by Ngombe craftsmen of the Democratic Republic of Congo, known as the Belgian Congo in the 1920s. Such pieces based on designs from "exotic" places and cultures were very popular during the Art Deco period. Doucet owned other pieces of African-inspired furniture by Legrain. ■

PIERRE LEGRAIN
French, 1889–1929

Tabouret, ca. 1923
Lacquer, wood, gilding, horn
20 ½ x 10 ½ x 25 ¼ in. (52 x 26.6 x
64.1 cm)
Sydney and Frances Lewis Endowment
Fund, 92.5

LOUIS MARCOUSSIS
Polish (active in France), 1883–1941
Made by MAISON MYRBOR
French (Paris) and Algerian, active
ca. 1910–ca. 1929

Carpet, ca. 1925
Wool
99 x 55 in. (252 x 140 cm)
Gift of Sydney and Frances Lewis, 85.343

Fig. 27: Entrance hall at Jacques Doucet's
Studio Saint-James, Neuilly, France.
L'Illustration (Paris, May 1930)

After studying in Cracow, Poland, and at the Académie Julian in Paris, illustrator and printmaker Louis Marcoussis was introduced to the Cubist painters Georges Braque and Pablo Picasso, who influenced his art. Certain elements such as the geometric shapes in the design of this carpet are emblematic of Cubism. The carpet was placed in the entrance hall on the ground floor (fig. 27) of Jacques Doucet's Studio Saint-James in Neuilly, a suburb of Paris. ▪

Jean Puiforcat, the leading Art Deco silversmith in France, began his career after the end of World War I in the studio of his family's firm. His designs show his interest in geometric forms such as circles and ovals. The silver objects he displayed at the 1925 Exposition Internationale des Arts Décoratifs et Industriels Modernes in Paris were a huge success and established his reputation as a progressive artist.

In 1929 he was one of the founding members of the avant-garde Union des Artistes Modernes (Union of Modern Artists), a group dedicated to the design of useful objects for mass production. His later silver was celebrated at the 1937 Exposition Internationale des Arts et Techniques dans la Vie Moderne in Paris, where he had his own pavilion and showed a tea service identical to this example. VMFA also has a silver vase by Puiforcat; it was first exhibited at the Salon of the Société des Artistes Décorateurs in Paris in 1928, and retailed at Saks Fifth Avenue in New York City.

JEAN PUIFORCAT
French, 1897–1945
Made by PUIFORCAT ORFÈVRE
French (Paris), founded 1820

Tea Service, 1937
Silver, rosewood
Coffeepot: 5 3/8 x 7 x 4 in. (13.1 x 17.8 x 10.1 cm)
Creamer: 3 x 4 3/4 x 3 1/8 in. (7.6 x 12 x 7.9 cm)
Sugar bowl: 3 x 4 1/2 x 3 1/8 in. (7.6 x 11.4 x 7.9 cm)
Teapot: 5 3/8 x 7 x 4 in. (13.1 x 17.8 x 10.1 cm)
Tray: 1 1/2 x 34 x 9 in. (3.8 x 86.4 x 22.9 cm)
Marked (each piece, under handle, bottom, and on side): maker's mark and hallmark
Gift of Sydney and Frances Lewis, 85.295.1–5

CLÉMENT ROUSSEAU
French, 1872–1950

Two Chairs, ca. 1925
Rosewood, sharkskin, mother-of-pearl,
replacement fabric
36 ½ x 17 x 20 ½ in. (92.7 x 43.2 x 52.1 cm)
(each)
Inscribed (inside front of seat frame): *Clement
Rousseau*
Gift of Sydney and Frances Lewis, 85.128–29

Clément Rousseau was a highly regarded Art Deco designer in Paris, and his sculpture and furniture were displayed regularly at exhibitions during the 1920s. Today, however, examples of his work are rare. While similar in form, these two chairs by Rousseau have backs that are in fact quite different in design. The stylized flower petals, volutes, sunray patterns, and frames are of dyed-green and natural-gray sharkskin, a favorite material of Rousseau and other designers. ■

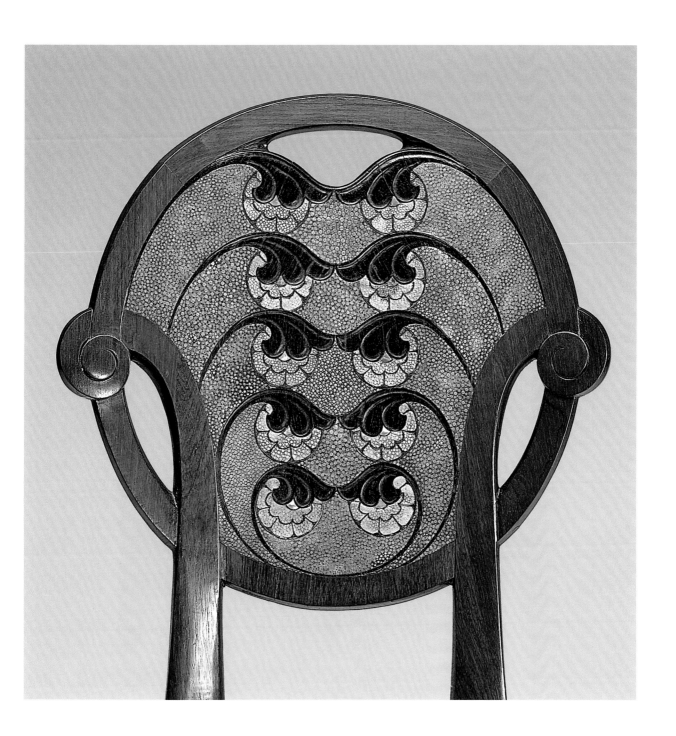

Émile-Jacques Ruhlmann's interior decoration and furnishings represent the height of French Art Deco elegance and luxury. During his short career—from 1910 to 1933—Ruhlmann set the fashion for wealthy and sophisticated patrons who valued his taste and refinement. As early as 1910, he displayed his designs at the Salon d'Autumne in Paris and followed with his first exhibition of furniture in 1913. By 1919 he had founded his firm with Pierre Laurent. Ruhlmann's pavilion, called the House of a Wealthy Collector, was one of the most important buildings at the 1925 Exposition Internationale des Arts Décoratifs et Industriels Modernes in Paris. It consisted of eight rooms that highlighted his interior decoration and furnishings as well as those of the many talented artists Ruhlmann hired to create this Art Deco masterpiece.

In his Paris workshops, Ruhlmann oversaw all aspects of interior decoration and luxury furniture production. He employed highly skilled artists and craftsmen who used only the finest and rarest materials: Makassar ebony was highlighted with ivory and silvered bronze mounts; drawers were embellished with silk tassels or ivory pulls; and leather, snakeskin, sharkskin, and tortoiseshell complemented the warm, dark tones of the wood.

This corner cupboard, made by Adolphe Chaneux and Gilbert Pelletier, is among Ruhlmann's most refined pieces. The ivory design on the door represents a vase, inspired by eighteenth-century forms, which Ruhlmann often featured in his furniture designs. Ivory was also used elsewhere to ornament the cabinet; for example, the door is framed with small ivory dots. A similar corner cupboard was displayed at the Ruhlmann retrospective exhibition in Paris in 1934. Today, there are only a few such cabinets in existence.

ÉMILE-JACQUES RUHLMANN
French, 1879–1933
Made by ADOLPHE CHANEUX
French, 1887–1965
Made by GILBERT PELLETIER
French, dates unknown
Made for RUHLMANN ET LAURENT
French (Paris), 1919–1933

Corner Cabinet, designed 1916, made ca. 1924
Makassar ebony, mahogany, rosewood, ebony, ivory, amaranth, brass
50 ½ x 33 ½ x 23 ¾ in. (128.3 x 85.1 x 60.3 cm)
Marked (bottom, rear edge): *Ruhlmann* (twice); (front, left top edge): *CP*
Gift of Sydney and Frances Lewis, 85.135

ÉMILE-JACQUES RUHLMANN
French, 1879–1933
Made by RUHLMANN ET LAURENT
French (Paris), 1919–1933

Desk, ca. 1925–27
Makassar ebony over oak, snakeskin, ivory, silvered bronze
28 ½ x 53 x 28 ½ in. (72.4 x 134.6 x 72.4 cm)
Inscribed (each drawer, bottom): *Ruhlmann B*
Gift of Sydney and Frances Lewis, 85.136.
Conservation funded by John and Maria Shugars

Émile-Jacques Ruhlmann regularly used Makassar ebony in his furniture. A rare striped wood, it is indigenous to Indonesia and named after the port town of Makassar. This desk, a tour de force of cabinetmaking, is unique in its design, craftsmanship, and beauty. The exotic snakeskin on the writing surface and the central drawer complements the grain of the ebony on the desktop and drawer fronts. Ruhlmann's furniture is noted for its superior cabinetmaking and finish as well as sophisticated detailing. VMFA has nine pieces of furniture and a rug by Ruhlmann. ■

In 1930 Jane Renouardt, a well-known French stage actress and the director of the Théâtre Daunou in Paris, purchased this bed from Émile-Jacques Ruhlmann for her house in Saint Cloud. Known as the *Sun Bed*, it is veneered in polished Makassar ebony over oak. The excellent crafts-manship of Ruhlmann's furniture is evident in the dramatic pattern of the headboard. The company's records note that one particular employee worked 252 ½ hours on the bed, which cost 11,375 francs—an exorbitant amount equal to about half of a craftsman's annual salary. Executed in June 1930 in studio B at Ruhlmann's firm, the *Sun Bed* was later moved from Saint Cloud to Renouardt's apartment in Paris at 24 avenue Gabriel.

A second *Sun Bed*, similar to the museum's example but lacking the two built-in side tables, was also made for Renouardt and her husband, Fernand Gravey. The fox fur on the museum's bed is a later addition. A similarly extravagant piece of furniture made for Renouardt, an ebony and mother-of-pearl cabinet by Süe et Mare, is also in VMFA's collection.

ÉMILE-JACQUES RUHLMANN
French, 1879–1933
Headboard made by JULES DEROUBAIX
French, dates unknown
Made by RUHLMANN ET LAURENT
French (Paris), 1919–1933

Sun Bed, designed 1923, made 1930
Makassar ebony over oak
77 x 83 ½ x 85 ¾ in. (195.6 x 212.1 x 217.8 cm)
Marked (headboard, back): *Ruhlmann;* (footboard, back): *Ruhlmann* (twice); (footboard, bottom): B
Gift of Sydney and Frances Lewis, 85.130

ÉDOUARD-MARCEL SANDOZ
Swiss (active in France), 1881–1971
Cast by C. VALSUANI
French (Chatillion and Paris),
1899–1970

Condor, ca. 1911–12
Bronze
14 ¼ x 21 ⅝ x 8 in (36.20 x 54.93 x
20.32 cm)
Marked (base, back left): *Ed. M. SANDOZ,
C. Valsuani*
Gift of S. Joel Schur, 2005.48

Édouard-Marcel Sandoz made several versions of his *Condor* in marble, bronze, and bronze with other metals. With different examples exhibited at the Salon of the Société des Artistes Décorateurs in Paris in 1912 and many other sites, *Condor* became well known and is today considered an icon of Art Deco sculpture. The size and bold appearance of this work convey the power of the bird. ◾

RAYMOND TEMPLIER
French, 1891–1968
Made by MAISON PAUL ET FILS
or MAISON PAUL ET RAYMOND
TEMPLIER
French (Paris)

Bracelet with Brooch, ca. 1925–30
Silver, platinum, gold, onyx, diamonds
2 1/8 x 2 1/4 x 2 1/2 in. (53.0 x 58.0 x
64.0 cm)
Marked: (bracelet, under brooch):
RAYMOND TEMPLIER; (bracelet, edge):
30141; (brooch, back): hallmarks, *30141*
Gift of the Sydney and Frances Lewis
Foundation, 85.257a–b

Raymond Templier, intrigued by modern technology, designed exceptionally fine Art Deco jewelry. In 1922 he joined the family firm, established by his paternal grandfather, Charles, in Paris in 1849. In addition, Templier held several official positions in the field of jewelry: vice president of the Salon d'Autumne in Paris, member of the board of the Association of Jewelers and Goldsmiths, and a founding member of the Union des Artistes Modernes. He also designed jewelry for the actress Brigitte Helm for the 1928 film *L'Argent* by Marcel L'Herbier. The central element of VMFA's impressive bracelet, which typifies Templier's use of abstract patterns and bold, geometric shapes, is a detachable brooch.

In 1919 architect-designer Louis Süe and painter-decorator André Mare established the Compagnie des Arts Français, known as Süe et Mare. With talented artists and designers on staff, the firm became well known for beautiful interiors and furniture. In 1924 Süe designed a house for the popular French stage actress Jane Renouardt, and Süe et Mare decorated and furnished it with sumptuous works of art, including this cabinet in ebony and mother-of-pearl. The form was directly inspired by Parisian eighteenth-century rococo furniture. ▪

LOUIS SÜE
French, 1875–1968
ANDRÉ MARE
French, 1885–1932
Made by COMPAGNIE DES ARTS FRANÇAIS
French (Paris), 1919–1928

Cabinet, ca. 1925
Ebony, mother-of-pearl, silver
61 ⅞ x 35 ⅜ x 15 ¾ in. (156.6 x 89.8 x 40 cm)
Marked (back, on paper label): *Chenue Emballeur, 5 Rue de la Terrasse Paris*
Gift of the Sydney and Frances Lewis Foundation, 85.137

INDEX

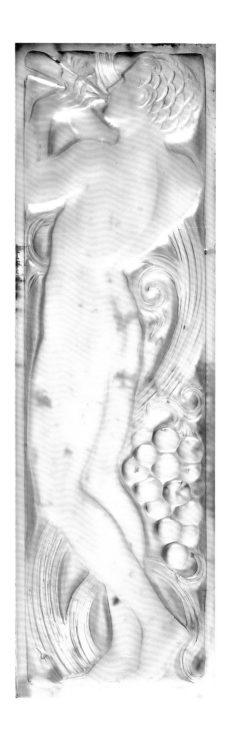